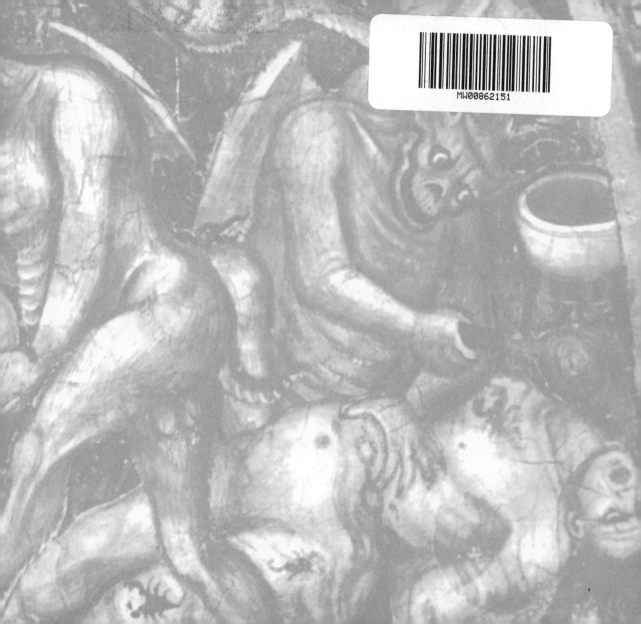

The Devil

THE

Devil

A Visual Guide to the Demonic,
Evil, Scurrilous, and Bad

CHRONICLE BOOKS
SAN FRANCISCO

Printed in Hong Kong.

ISBN 0-8118-1176-X

Library of Congress Cataloging-in-Publication Data available.

Book and cover design: Blue Design, San Francisco, CA.

Distributed in Canada by Raincoast Books,
8680 Cambie Street
Vancouver, BC V6P 6M9

10 9 8 7 6 5 4 3 2 1

Chronicle Books
275 Fifth Street
San Francisco, CA 94103

Page 2: Lucifer reigns over the souls of sinners, from an illustration by John Baptist Medina, 1688

Page 6: Saint Francis of Borgia Exorcising a Demonized Dying Man, Francisco de Goya y Lucientes, 1788

Page 9: Devil Dog © William Wegman, 1990. Courtesy PaceWildensteinMacGill Gallery, New York, New York.

PLEASED TO MEET YOU,
HOPE YOU GUESS MY NAME...

CONTENTS

THERE IS NO HEAD SO HOLY THAT THE DEVIL DOES NOT MAKE A NEST IN IT.

Introduction

"The Devil's cleverest wile is to make men believe that he does not exist."

GERALD C. TREACY

The maxim *to hold a candle to the devil* alludes to an old Irish tale. One Feast of Saint Michael's day an elderly woman came to pay homage to the saint. As she did, she lit a candle for the conquered dragon, too. When her local priest asked the woman why she would do such a thing, the woman replied that she wasn't sure whether she'd be going up or down, to Heaven or Hell, after she died, so she'd better secure a friend in both places. It was this insecurity that inspired us to write a sequel to our first book, *Saints*, about the Devil, his legion of demons, and the lore that surrounds them. Whenever we mentioned that we were working on a book about cosmology's black sheep, we were inevitably greeted with surprise that there could be that much to write about. After all, the Devil seems straightforward enough and is, with that said, a topic

St. Michael evicting Lucifer and the fallen angels from heaven, by Albrecht Dürer from Apocalypse, 1498

11

better off avoided. It is arguably risky to steer one's course toward the dark side voluntarily, for one only has to mention the Devil and he manifests himself in one way or another—we were chaperoned during the writing of this book by a leering, cackling flock of ravens that roosted outside our window. We persevered, however, determined that it is better to know what one is up against after all, and besides, it is infinitely more fun to play with the bad guys.

But it is not easy to tread lightly on the subject of evil and its mythology. In writing this book, one thing became clear: the nature of wickedness and its incarnate representation, the Devil, are as slippery as a serpent in one's intellectual grasp. Great religious thinkers from Enoch to Saint Thomas Aquinas to more contemporary writers have struggled valiantly to construct workable theories to rationalize the existence of a benevolent God in light of the overwhelming suffering, maliciousness, and unjustifiable misery in the world. It would take several volumes larger than this to go into these individual theories in the depth they deserve, but we encourage anyone who is interested in the subject to pursue this study. It is riveting social history, philosophy, and prophecy, as relevant today as it ever has been. The thread that remains consistent in these ideas, however, is the acceptance that, at least for now, the Devil and his minions appear to have the upper hand in the dealings with mortals and the physical world they inhabit (because, most of these theoreticians would argue, God wants it that way).

Seal of Lucifer

The devil tempts all, but the idle man tempts the devil.

The Devil in repose, 15th century

1 2

And so here we have the being known by a thousand names, the absolute incarnation of evil, the emperor of the realm of grief: Lucifer, the angel of God, whose pride sparked a war that rent the Heavens and caused no end of misery to the human race. Satan, the adversary, who accuses and punishes sinners, toting their souls off in a sack to languish in cauldrons of liquid fire. The Devil, a being of consummate complexity, the supreme ruler of chaos and discord, who is bound in Hell by the power of Christ. Mephistopheles, the personification of cultured vice, who slyly seduces his victims with sophistication and wit, only to tear them limb from limb as he devours their souls. The Archfiend answers to all of the above; and we humans, to our utter misfortune, are his only occupation. The Devil's primary objective is to be worshipped by humanity as a god, to rival his estranged parent in the minds of men and to create a dominion equal to that of Heaven. To that end, he enlists hordes of demons and damned souls to do his bidding, leading men down the path of iniquity and through the one-way gates of Hell.

Mephistopheles

Lucifer devouring Brutus, Cassius, and Judas Iscariot, 1512

Popular characterizations of the Western European Devil do not appear in art or writing until the sixth century, a good two hundred years after Christianity became the region's accepted religion. It was not until the Middle Ages, that epoch of manic superstition and fear, that the Archfiend and his legions grew to their ferocious stature in human history. As they percolated up through the darker sides of human nature, the attributes of evil spawned an eclectic mix of demonized pagan icons and outright attacks on competing religious beliefs. Because Christianity's success relied on the conversion of believers from their native religions, the Christian idea of evil subverts all other religions, turning them into blasphemy spewed from the mouth of the evil one himself. Yet it is precisely this amalgamation of ancient beliefs and biases that has led to the fascinating mythology that surrounds the Prince of Woe. Because of this abundant well of ideas, writing, and artwork, this book primarily discusses the Western European Devil and his legends, as derived from the Judeo-Christian canon. It is interesting to note that the Devil is hardly mentioned in the Old and New Testament. The stories and representations commonly associated with the Devil, including the fall of Lucifer, are apocryphal and have evolved from ancient Hebrew and early Gnostic beliefs. However, devils, demons, and evil spirits exist in all countries and in the history of every religion. In some cases we have attempted to touch upon them, but in no way are they paid their proper respect.

In addition to the legends and lore surrounding the Devil, we have also included a journey into Hell. A basic listing of rebel angels and demons will help you find your way around. For those who want to enjoy the friendship of the Fiend vicariously, without the threat of eternal damnation, we have added stories of mortals—witches, sorcerers, and the

Face of Satan,
German, 17th century

Ego ſum Papa.

"I am the Pope,"
from a Reformation
handbill, 15th century

like—who have sold their souls. We encourage you to read these accounts before acting rashly; because once sold, a soul is nearly impossible to redeem. If you are already in the unfortunate position of having made such a bargain and you are looking for a way out, see our first book, *Saints*. There may be somebody in there who can help you. If you are being hounded by impure spirits, the last chapter in this book will reveal some different ways to repel them.

It is impossible to discuss the Devil without broaching the subject of racism and hatred. Due to our focus on the mythological aspects of the Devil, the tales in this book do not incorporate the very real brutal persecutions that transpired in the name of God throughout history. Early Christians found Satan under every stone, in every pagan temple or Jewish synagogue, even amidst their own brethren. How else could they explain the enmity, persecution, and divisiveness they too experienced? Schooled in the art of grandstand torture by the Romans, later Christians could be quite ruthless in routing out children of the Devil, as evidenced by the Crusades, the Inquisition, and the witch trials. Jewish and Gnostic sects were particularly subject to persecution and demonization—Jews for the part they allegedly played in the Crucifixion and Gnostics because their competing gospels threatened to topple Christianity's shaky foundation. Unfortunately, the discrimination against Jews has not lost its voracity. Many of the common attributes we associate with the Devil are actually vicious caricatures of medieval Jews. Hatred and discrimination do not begin or end with the Christians, however; it seems that every group from

The Devil always leaves a stink behind him.

Fall of the Rebel Angels. Lucifer and his legions are expelled from Heaven, by Gustave Doré, 19th-century engraving for Paradise Lost.

1 9

the dawn of time until the present day has judged and found wanting others who do not look or talk like them, or believe precisely what they believe. Apparently evil is not the exclusive domain of the Devil; we humans have learned well and established our own flourishing fiefdom here

Martin Luther depicted as the instrument of the devil in an anti-Reformation handbill, 16th century

on earth. One last caveat of this nature: in our effort to present the myths surrounding damnation, it was necessary simply to describe the characterizations as they evolved in popular history; we made no allowances for many contemporary groups who may categorize themselves as Satanists, witches, sorcerers, or magicians but who pose no threat to society and are hurt by the insinuation. It is not our intent to further malign these groups, but to discuss the imagery and legend that has grown up around them—some of which is so ludicrous as to be entirely self-evident.

It is impossible to know whether or not the Devil and the misery he has caused humanity will be vanquished in the near future. All we can be sure of is that the more we struggle to resist temptation, the better off we will be. It is wise to remember that the Devil and his legions may only *tempt* humans to sin. There is a choice. Perhaps upon reading this volume, with its descriptions of the atrocities that can befall a wayward soul, it will be easier to understand the Devil and thus evade the many pitfalls his demons dig along our path to righteousness. If worse comes to worse, you might as well follow the example of the old woman in the Irish legend and hedge your bets, because no one knows for sure whether they are going up or down. We'll say one thing after becoming students of the Devil for a short while. We pray it is up.

Genevieve and Tom Morgan

DEVIL'S NIGHT (OCTOBER 30) 1995

The Devil gets up the belfry by the vicar's skirts.

"How you are fallen from Heaven,
O Day Star, son of Dawn!
How you are cut down to the ground
you who laid the nations low!
You said in your heart,
'I will ascend to Heaven;
Above the stars of God
I will set my throne on high.'"
-ISAIAH 14:12-13

The Origin of Evil

The serpent approaches,
by Gustave Doré, 19th-
century engraving

From the first pantheistic religious celebrations worshipping natural spirits to the panoply of Greek and Roman gods to many Native American and Eastern religions still in practice today, deities were and are thought to be whimsical, mercurial forces that offer prosperity and grace to believers as arbitrarily as they do destruction and death. The principles of good (creation) and evil (negation) in these beliefs are not two separate entities, but combine as opposing facets of a deity's personality, just as the propensity for good or for evil are extant in a human's psyche. It is a relatively rare tenet in religion to pin the misery of the human condition on one being. In fact, the only four major religions that have proffered belief in a single personification of evil are all monotheistic: Christianity, Islam, ancient Judaism, and Zoroastrianism. As monotheism began to compete with pantheism in many regions (as early as 700 B.C. in Persia

2 3

and some other countries), the concept of evil began to change. The evolution is clear in the Bible: The Hebrew God of the Old Testament, Yahweh, still harbors some residual ambiguity in his nature. When displeased, he is quite capable of inflicting (and at times appears eager to inflict) great misery by hardening hearts or sending his angels of destruction to rain fire on his human subjects. Evil in the Old Testament is the result of sin. Human beings were sinners and God chose to have them punished. Although other religions (including many Gnostic religions) held that evil was a separate, equally powerful entity from the divine, present before the cosmos was created, most monotheistic believers promoted the idea that wickedness and despair were adjuncts of God. They were the nasty underbelly of Paradise, because nothing could exist without God calling it into being.

By the fourth century (when it was legalized), Christianity came clamoring to the forefront of Western European religion, and with it, the doctrine that the one and only true God is the absolute essence of pure love and goodness. To suggest that a mean or selfish vibration emanated from his holy visage was an outrage to true believers, but the early Christian theologians were left with a burning question: If God is love, they pondered, then who or what is responsible for evil? Thus began the extrapolation of many ideas and the evolution of popular superstitions and myths that evolved into what some consider to be one of the richest strains of thought ever to surface in human history—the mythic story of how the Devil and his legions of woe came to be.

Persian Demon

Early Assyrian demons

Satan contemplates his predicament, by Gustave Doré, 19th-century engraving

Lucifer

On the first day of the universe, God separated light from dark, morning from night. On the second day, he called into being the firmament of Heaven and populated it with entities of free will made of pure light—the nine choirs of angels—to keep him company in Heaven and serve as his vassals. Realizing that the angels might choose to do wrong because they were creatures of free will, God touched a portion of them with grace. The angels, made of an ethereal, shimmering substance and sporting wings that glistened with living gold, illuminated the halls and throne room of the Divine; but none shined so brightly as the Angel of the Morning, God's left-hand man: Lucifer, Son of Dawn.

Lucifer was a cherub of the highest order, a Seraphim with six wings. One of God's first creations, his dazzling beauty, power, and grace made

him a favorite. The Creator positioned his most beautiful angel directly
to his lower left, where he would be free to gaze down upon Lucifer's
benevolent countenance. As if this tribute weren't enough, God also
bestowed upon Lucifer dominion over earth, which up to that point
was his most treasured creation. Lucifer received these honors as befit-
ting an angel of his rank and thanked his benefactor with the appropriate hosannas. Lucifer took his seat of power and began to marvel at the

The Etruscan demon,
Tuchulcha

magnitude of his own authority. He pondered why a being such as he had to answer to anyone at all. Why must he hold God's son, or for that matter, God, above himself? The cherub raised his hand to his chin and grew distracted by the sheer beauty of his being. Again he ominously turned his thoughts from his Creator to himself. Lucifer questioned why he was sitting lower than God if he was so powerful, so beautiful. Surely a superlative creature such as he was worthy of his own kingdom; to be like God, subservient to no one—now that was real power.

As these damning thoughts whirled around the ill-fated angel's head, Lucifer's first daughter, Sin, took a woeful leap from his forehead. As if on cue, the Divine Father rose from his throne to check on the latest holy invention: a man named Adam fashioned from dirt and clay in the Lord's image. Lucifer felt a stab of jealousy at the thought of this new creation. Would Adam usurp his esteemed position in God's eyes? Envy commingled with vanity, ambition with pride, and a nest of vipers grew in Lucifer's bold and careless heart.

> *Hell is paved with good intentions.*
> SAMUEL JOHNSON

The Fall

With the holy throne empty, Lucifer grabbed the opportunity and ascended to seat himself on his Creator's chair. As his cherubic brethren faced him, Lucifer proclaimed that *he* was their new leader and would offer them more than the other ever could. After all, he reasoned to the angels, they were creatures of free will, able to worship one god as well as the next. Bored by their liturgical duties and swayed by delusions of grandeur, a full third of the angels populating the choirstalls (a fifteenth-century Bishop of Tusculum estimated 133,306,668 angels in all) bowed down to the impostor. Lucifer swelled with triumph. He and the rebel angels proceeded to set up their own rival kingdom, described in John Milton's epic poem *Paradise Lost* as located in the north of Heaven. The outraged Archangel Michael rallied the remaining two-thirds of the angels to arms. They waged a terrible war against the insubordinates, intent on driving them from Heaven. Finally, on what some imagined to be August first (a date referred to in *Paradise Lost*), after a day of vicious battle, God returned from the Garden of Eden to see his precious Lucifer seated defiantly on his throne, ruling his fool's paradise. To the shame of his Creator, Lucifer's wings, once glistening, now burned with the false flame of his sins. Before God's eyes, his beloved angels tore one another to pieces. When God saw what Lucifer had done, his wrath had no mercy. With one hefty stroke, Lucifer and the rebel angels were hurled from the divine presence for eternity, their pure, shining bodies turning black and oily as they rained down from Heaven.

Archangel Michael conquers Satan

In the Muslim tradition, the Qur'an relates a more troubling, ambiguous version of the same tale. Lucifer (known as Iblis before the Fall and Shaytan after) rebels against God (Allah) because of pride.

When Allah brings Adam in front of the angels, he demands that each angel bow down in front of his new creation. When he reaches Iblis, the Angel of Morning asks, "Why should I, a son of fire, bow down before a son of clay?" God's reaction is swift and decisive, and the disobedient angel is expelled from heaven. In a Sufi rendition of the same story, Lucifer does not bow down before Adam because he loves his God so much that to worship anything else would be sacrilege. He thinks he *is* obeying God by abiding his preexisting command to never bow down before false idols. Either God misunderstands Lucifer's devoted stance (which is hard to believe) or he has made the decision to allow Lucifer to fall and intentionally sets up this catch-22.

Lucifer and his companions fell like bricks for nine long days. When they finally struck the ground the massive weight of their sins broke the surface of the earth, which opened like a set of massive jaws in a great, shuddering yawn. Lucifer and his legion toppled headfirst into the fire and brimstone of the Abyss, located in some beliefs at the exact center of the earth. No longer the angel of light, Lucifer became known forevermore as the Devil. The primordial sinner with no hope of salvation, he was sentenced to burn in Hell for all time. Frothing at the mouth with rage, the Devil swore to the legion of angels he had brought down with him that he would turn the slop-heap of Hell into a kingdom to challenge Heaven, a princedom dedicated to opposing all that God, in his goodness, intended. Thus, fallen from grace, devoid of good, and bound in duty to chaos and darkness, Lucifer and the rebel angels bore evil into the world.

*The War in Heaven.
Michael defeats Lucifer
and the rebel army, by
Gustave Doré, 19th-
century engraving*

3 1

Satan and Original Sin

Bereft of his favorite vassal and a full third of his angels, God optimistically turned his hopes to his new creation. He visited Adam in the Garden of Eden and created Eve. (In an old Jewish tradition, the Devil actually came from the wound created in Adam's flesh when God took his rib to make Eve.) God commanded the pair to be fruitful and multiply so that they, in turn, could procreate enough blissful children to re-populate the empty choirstalls in Heaven; but it was not to be. Satan, the dastardly fiend (who is believed to be the Devil himself or his second-in-command depending on which tradition you read), set about ruining God's plan. What better way to get back at his conqueror than to pervert these innocent beings and turn them away from God? Assuming the shape of a serpent (the symbol for the devourer of light in Asia), the Devil entered the Garden of Eden and tempted Eve to sin. Eve, also a being with free will, bit into the forbidden fruit because the Devil deluded her by convincing her she would be like a god if she did. Once the fruit's flesh was in her mouth, the Devil tricked her by creating false visions of wisdom and grandeur. She ran to Adam to share the wonder she had just experienced and asked him to partake of the fruit, too. He complied with little hesitation, and the rest, as they say, is history. Because of this mighty trespass, God surrendered his freshly minted humans to the Devil and reluctantly delivered their progeny to sin and death.

From the moment Adam and Eve tasted the flesh of forbidden fruit, they alienated themselves from God and painted all mankind with the

The devil of conceit rides a woman's coattails, 15th century

> If God lived on earth, people would break His windows.

brush of Original Sin. Because of their disobedience in the Garden, all humans are *born* sinners. Living under the yoke of the Devil in life, humanity would know pain and suffering and death—all unfamiliar concepts in Eden—and, to top it off, *all* souls would now rot in Hell under the control of the Unholy One. Because of Original Sin, the pearly gates were shut and locked to the likes of man, *never to be opened again.* Adam and Eve were banished to a world decidedly less attractive than Paradise. God would have to look elsewhere to repopulate his empty choirstalls; and Satan, his mission complete, must have giggled maniacally to himself as he slithered back to his cohorts in Hell, content that, in one fell swoop, he had doomed the human race to suffer his torments for eternity.

Christ and Salvation

If one believes the Christians, however, we are not without hope even though we are all born sinners. In all fairness, God probably realized that he could have made Adam and Eve more resistant to temptation, so in his unknowable kindness, God in essence delivered *himself* to the Devil in order to redeem his wretched creation by manifesting his holiness in the mortal flesh of Jesus Christ. This is the concept of the Holy Trinity: the Father, the Son, and the Holy Ghost are united in one eternal godhead that has always existed, each branch of the trinity being equally divine. Jesus Christ, the Lord incarnate, came to earth and sacrificed himself to

The Last Judgment *(detail), by Fra Angelico, circa 1420*

3 4

save mankind from unequivocal damnation. Born a mortal in the flesh of his son, God experienced firsthand the horror of the human condition and set a snare for his archenemy. The Devil presumed that Jesus was just a simple man; he had no idea he was up against someone who was divine and *sinless* (not tainted by Original Sin). Overconfident at the sight of the wandering prophet, the Devil was convinced he could win over this second Adam and turn him to the ways of wickedness.

While Jesus was in the desert, Satan approached him in the guise of a broken old man. He offered Christ illusions of unchecked power and wealth and tempted him to test his faith in God by jumping to his death off a high wall. "If God is as powerful as you say he is," the Devil baited, "then he won't let you die." In some versions, the Prince of Evil even lifts Christ onto his shoulder, offering him the reins of a kingdom that stretched as far as the eye could see. But Jesus, who knew that all the Devil could offer was lies, refused temptation and chased the Devil away. The Prince of Woe, quite alarmed by the backbone of this man, scurried back to Hell to consult with his cabinet. Infuriated at his failure, the Archfiend schemed to show this irritating do-gooder what real power was all about. In his frenzy for revenge, the Devil arranged the persecution, betrayal, and crucifixion of Christ. But because Jesus was not guilty of sin, he was unjustly punished. The Devil, by recklessly and wrongly ordering him to be tortured and killed, lost his undisputed dominion over human souls. Christians believe that Christ died to redeem mankind, that we are no

Jesus casting out the devil. After a painting by Schnorr von Carolsfeld

longer doomed to Hell because of Original Sin. God's sacrifice gave each of us a chance for salvation; the heavens, if we behave ourselves, may once again be opened to admit mankind.

The Harrowing of Hell

In a continuation of the story espoused by many Christian sects, after Christ's death and before the Resurrection, his soul journeys to Hell to free the virtuous souls who had died before he was able to save them. Accompanied by the sound of triumphant angels singing in celebration at the imminent deposition of evil, Jesus commands the gates of Hell to open before him. Upon entering, Jesus sees Satan, the Prince of Hell, and Beelzebub, the Prince of Death, fighting in the hallway. He curses them both and they let him pass. He fights with the Devil and is victorious. In some legends, the Devil is bound by chains to a gridiron for a thousand years. In others, he is vanquished but not bound. As Christ departs, he frees all the souls who were prisoners of Hell and locks the Devil's motley crew in the bowels of Hell. The procession joyously ascends out of Hell. Some creeds believe that the souls were deposited in Limbo (see Hell and Damnation, page 59), others claim they were allowed through the pearly gates. The Devil, gnashing his teeth in despair, cries foul upon seeing he has been robbed of his infernal population and demands that he still be allowed dibs on the souls of sinners and unbelievers. God relents and grants him this power until Judgment Day when Christ is supposed to return and the Devil and all who follow him will be banished from the world forever.

Christ journeys to Hell and frees the souls held prisoner there

Farewell happy Field;
Where Joy for ever dwells, Hail horrors, hail
Infernal world, and thou profoundest Hell
Receive thy new Possessor.

MILTON, FROM *PARADISE LOST*

The Prince of Darkness

Please allow me to introduce myself,
I'm a man of wealth and taste
I've been around for a long long year
Laid many a man's soul to waste.

MICK JAGGER/KEITH RICHARDS

And so, far afield from his glorious post on high, we find the once proud and mighty Lucifer suffering the ultimate demotion. His once beautiful visage is now distorted into a waxen, leathery mask; his former heavenly body is a repulsive, misshapen hide. The absolute embodiment of evil, the Devil festers forevermore in the Hell of his making; but his predicament has not stemmed the diabolical flow of corruption, sin, and vice he orders unleashed on the earth. He has hordes of servants commanded by his army of rebel angels to do his bidding and is able to make the occasional visit himself, albeit by possessing some hapless soul. His name is legion, his wretchedness unequaled, his countenance uglier than anything a mere mortal could describe; yet many have attempted through the ages to capture the unique monstrosity of the

Lucifer, *by Jacopo Tintoretto (detail from* The Temptation of Christ)

4 1

*Few are saved,
infinitely more are
damned.*
MARTIN LUTHER

Archfiend. The Devil, or at least how he chooses to show himself, is now an instantly recognizable character due to the surfeit of illustration and description that continues to this very day.

There is no known depiction of the Devil before the sixth century. Christianity was recognized in Europe in the fourth century, and it seems to have taken a couple of centuries for Lucifer and his legions to show their countenances. When they did, it was in the form of small, black, impish figures. As the notion of evil and its creator grew in power and status during the Middle Ages, depictions of the Devil became increasingly revolting and, ironically, more and more human. By the dawn of the Age of Enlightenment, Christian images of Lucifer had matured from a primordial shadow to a sophisticated, duplicitous entity with the ability to appear as a dashing young man, an angel of light, or a slathering, blood-sucking beast. In our secular society today, demonic power is often depicted as alien, mechanical, or robotic—technology gone awry—with the Devil possessing inanimate objects like houses, lawnmowers, and cars. Nevertheless, when the human imagination throughout the ages has dared to dwell on the Dark One, classic themes have consistently emerged. Much of the attributes popularly associated with the Devil are actually demonized facets of pagan and other non-Christian religions, images subverted by the early Christian fathers to help their nascent religion gain solid ground.

*Lucifer lands in Hell,
by Gustave Doré, 19th-
century engraving*

Names

The Devil is a being of infinite forms that has almost as many names. The word *devil* is derived indirectly from the Greek word *diabolos*, meaning slanderer, which appears in ancient Hebrew texts. Devil and Satan have become synonymous; but Satan comes from the Hebrew word *satan,* meaning adversary, and he acts as the opposing angel in the Old Testament. The satan was not associated with a principle of evil, but with God. In fact, Satan in the Old Testament was a messenger of God. Although some strains of religious thought differentiate between the Devil and Satan as distinct entities, the Prince of Darkness or any of his peers will answer to any of the following: Abbadon, Apollyon, Ascmedai, Asmodeus, Baal, Beelzebub, Belial, Demon, Devil, Dragon, Leviathan, Lucifer, Mephistopheles, Sammael, Satan, or Serpent.

Many cultures believed that one risked the possibility of beckoning the Devil by speaking his name, so a host of euphemistic appellations evolved. Of the several hundred, some of the most common are: The Baker (because he pops sinners in the oven to roast), the Stoker (fueling the fires of Hell), the Poker, Diablo (Spanish), Diable (Italian), Teufel (German), Tempter, Old Hairy, Old Horny, Bogeyman, Old Bogie, the Deceiver of Mankind, Archfiend, Dark Prince, Black Jack, Horny Jack, Lusty Dick, the Accuser, the Fallen Star of Morning, the Apostate, the Old Gentleman, Gentleman Jack, the Black Dog, the Prince of the Pit, the Potentate of the Pit, and Dickens. When

*The Trinity
of Evil*

*Lucifer's argument with
the deity, from an early
11th-century manuscript*

4 5

you send someone to the Dickens or to the Deuce, you are actually damning them to Hell.

In a twisted version of the Santa Claus legend, the Devil is referred to as "Old Nick." In this story, the Evil One lives in the North and drives reindeer. He wears a red suit and gets into people's homes through the chimney. He carries a large sack into which he tosses sinners and, with particular glee, naughty children. He flies through the air and is appeased with offerings of wine and food. The connection between Santa Claus and the Devil may be nothing more than a Victorian attempt to demonize Santa Claus because the Christmas festivities struck them as too pagan in nature. Nonetheless, children were warned to be good as gold or else Old Nick or the Christmas Devil, also known as Krumpus, would visit instead of Santa Claus and tote them off to Hell.

15th-century Satan

Forms

As a polymorphous figure, the Devil can take the form of any being or possess any unsuspecting entity he wishes, from masquerading as an angel of light or the Virgin Mary to assuming the form of an animal, insect, or occasionally, an inanimate object. The following descriptions have evolved in popular imagination from a wealth of literary and artistic sources. From early Christian legends to medieval mystery plays to the artwork of Goya and Brueghel, the Devil continues to be a common subject and is now a universally recognized

Devils and demons bicker at the mouth of Hell

entity. In the most widespread, generic descriptions of the Dark Prince, he is usually male (although he freely takes the form of an irresistible woman, especially when he visits monks). He often appears gargantuan and deformed, his inner defamation manifesting itself externally. He walks with a limp caused by his tumble from Heaven, and his knees are backwards. He is occasionally depicted with three heads in a perversion of the Holy Trinity, and he may possess another face on his distended belly or backside.

In a demonization of the Greco-Roman satyr Pan, the Devil is said to be covered with thick, oily hair. He sports horns, cloven hooves, and a tail. If the Fiend still has his wings, they are reptilian and grotesque. His eyes are fathomless dark pits sunk in a cadaverous face. He owns only one nostril, out of which he shoots flames. In Hebrew legend, the Devil has twelve wings and is covered in eyes. In other traditions, he has seven heads, ten horns, and seven crowns on his head. He vomits blasphemy and constantly belches and farts sulfurous air, which rises into the world from the sooty fires he stokes in Hell and encourages people to sin. He gnaws relentlessly on the bodies of sinners, their entrails mixing with his spittle to create a bloody froth that drips down his chin. Once swallowed, the sinners are excreted through his anus, only to be picked up and devoured all over again.

When the Infernal One chooses to visit earth in the form of an animal, he prefers the shape of a serpent, dragon, ape, goat, or dog. He never appears as a lamb, an ass, or an ox, because these animals

Lucifer safety matches

were present at the birth of Jesus. The Devil's affinity for goats may allude to the ancient pagan deity Priapus, god of all vegetation and fertility (symbolized by his giant, erect phallus), whose sacred animal was a goat. The dragon was popular in medieval legends for embodying evil; in particular, its penchant for torching victims with its fiery breath was a habit that struck people as singularly demonic. The Devil is considered to be the original mimic—or, as the early cleric Tertullian claimed, "God's Ape"—perversely copying anything divine; and he is thus frequently depicted as a monkey. Occasionally, the Fiend transforms into an elephant with the feet of a bear (also the form of the demon Behemoth, see page 88) which could be a derogatory reference to Ganesha, the Hindu god of wisdom. Ravens, pigs, and bats are depicted as additional, although less frequent, manifestations. The raven draws its fiendish characteristic from its appearance in Scandinavian mythology, where the dark god Odin had two ravens on his shoulder. The bat appears because it is thought to be frighteningly ugly and is a creature of the night. Rodents are popular because of their association with witches and disease. The cat, although revered as a divine figure in ancient Egypt, was demonized and persecuted by medieval Christians. Cats were infrequently possessed by the Devil, but they were associated with witches, bad luck, and evil or hysterical women—thus the origin of the description *hell cat* and the superstition of never letting a black cat cross your path.

The serpent is the Devil's favorite form. In ancient Eastern religions, serpents were the gatekeepers of knowledge and great treasure, and this belief perhaps led to their appearance in Western traditions in which the Devil takes the form of the serpent to enter the Garden of Eden. As the tempter and enticer, the serpent is closely related to Christian ideas of women and sexuality. Synonymous with carnal knowledge and sensuality, the serpent was able to tempt Eve because, if you believe some early Christian artists and writers, like attracts like. For this reason, the serpent in Paradise is often drawn or depicted on stage as having a woman's head. In fact, early Christian writers, such as the Venerable Bede, promoted the idea that women and the Devil are synonymous (a belief that does not die hard, as evidenced by the witch trials). In this line of thought, God created Adam; and, to outdo him, the Devil created Eve. The temptation and the forbidden fruit of Original Sin are really a euphemism for Adam (thought and spirit) being seduced by Eve (matter and flesh), thus setting the stage for the eternal battle between spirit and flesh, mind and spleen, good and evil.

Attributes and Guises

Most of the icons associated with the Devil have their origin in fertility symbols. The shape of the pitchfork that the Devil uses to prod and torment sinners represents fertility in Hindu and Native American religions and may also be a carryover from the legend of Neptune's

> *Heaven has a road, but no one travels it; Hell has no gate, but men will bore through to get there.*

trident. The Devil's horns may be an emblem derived from the satyr Pan, but is more likely a reference to the untamed sexuality of bulls. The crescent moon turned sideways resembles horns; and, for this reason, the Fiend's horns may be a demonization of pagan moon worship. The moon is a symbol of fertility and the feminine, but it also connotes darkness and death. In Europe powerful people were often depicted with rays of light that resembled horns emanating from their forehead, a superstition that may have originated with bishops' mitres. In medieval times, the "horns of Moses" were associated with Jews, fueling the ongoing demonization of Jews; and powerful Jews in the community were depicted with horns, signifying their subservience to the Dark One. The Devil may also be shown carrying a fiery sword or rod, which he brandishes with relish. This symbol may allude to the war in Heaven, but more likely represents the Devil's virility and power.

Old Horny loves to appear as a clergy person. He easily adopts the robes of a priest and can thunder from the pulpit with the best of them. He also enjoys playing practical jokes on holy men and women, such as hiding their vestments or locking them in a confession booth while he performs Mass. A favorite trick of the Devil is to change newborn babies' faces to look exactly like the parish priest, thus causing a delightful ruckus in townships and the clergyman's humiliation.

In contemporary interpretations, the Devil visits humans in the guise of an attractive urbanite. More often than not, he uses the alias Mephistopheles, and he is a picture of up-to-date fashion and sophistication. This

manifestation of the Devil is all the more dangerous, because he may fool even the most educated individual. A master orator, philosopher, and academic, he is especially prone to masquerading as a scholar or teacher. He runs in only the finest social circles and makes a wonderful dinner guest as his conversation is always witty and ripe with gossip. Although he has succeeded in ridding himself of his more barbaric features, the Devil still has a tell-tale limp and the remnant of a tail that may give him away. If you confront the Fiend with the truth, his elaborate disguise will fall away and his true diabolical form will reveal itself. The Devil is thus the patron of lawyers and actors because they represent themselves falsely. The printing press and the publishing industry are associated with the Devil because he gave mankind the means to mass-produce the Bible and thus bastardized it. Catholic leaders saw the ability to disburse uncontrolled information would lead to a flood of corruption and wickedness via the printed word.

Diabolical Colors

In Northern European cultures, the Devil is generally black, symbolizing an absence of light and good. Black is symbolic of fear, the unknown, night, blindness, and chaos. It was also related to plagues (the Black Death), poison, the Underworld, and stupidity (or denseness). Occasionally the Prince of Darkness rides a black horse. Interestingly, devils in many Eastern and African religions are white, although much of the fear associated with a lack of light prevails. The Prince's relation

Hell, by Taddeo di Bartolo, 1396

to reptiles and the pagan deities of vegetation and fertility—such as the aforementioned Pan and Priapus, and the Green Man, the ancient European mythological figure that is a god of vegetation and forests—led some artists to depict him with green skin. Alternatively, the Devil's flesh is red, singed by the fires of Hell and stained by the blood of the sinners he devours. The Fiend usually dresses in black or red. His livery is black and yellow, the hues of disease, death, and quarantine. His affinity for red has led to the belief that redheaded or ruddy-skinned humans are more susceptible to his charms and may even be related to a demon. Blondes are not exempt either; the yellow of their hair attracts the Devil, and they are less likely to ward off his advances than brunettes. Blue is occasionally associated with the Devil, but it is the gaseous blue of a sulfur flame, not the sky blue of the Heavens.

The Devil shown covered with thick, oily hair and reptilian wings

The Infernal Family

The Devil has a powerful grandmother who may be Hecate, the mythological goddess of nature. In some legends, the Devil's mother is Lilith (see page 101), Adam's first wife. In other stories, Lilith is his whore and Cain is their son. She and the demons circle the Devil's throne singing hideous hymns to his glory. The Devil has other females in his vile harem: Nehema, Aggareth, Igymeth, and Machlath. The Prince of Hell holds himself up as an example in fornication, fathering seven daughters, each one espousing one of the seven deadly sins. He has incestuous relations with his first daughter, Sin, with whom he parented

the woe of mankind, Death. In addition, he is said to have engendered several hideous half-human offspring, including Attila the Hun. (It's been rumored that Voltaire and Baudelaire may have had diabolical origins, no doubt gossip spread by their competitors.)

Shakespeare's character Caliban in *The Tempest* is the progeny of the Devil and a witch. Merlin was allegedly the fruit of the Devil's copulation with a nun, but luckily the wizard took after his mother. The New Testament foretells that, in one final attempt to regain his power over humanity, the Devil will father one more child, a nefarious son bent on undoing the redemption guaranteed to mankind by Christ. This Antichrist will be born to the Devil and a Babylonian whore. He will herald himself as the Second Coming of Jesus and unleash the domination of evil over the world, but his vainglorious promises will be empty and only the nonbelievers will follow him. When the real Messiah comes, the false prophet and his blasphemous congregation will be cast out for eternity, while the virtuous will ascend the Golden Ladder to take their place with the angels.

The Hell Hunt and Other Favorite Haunts

For entertainment, the Devil often rallies a few demons together and takes them out into the forest at night to hunt. As the Devil furiously rides his undead steed backward in his saddle through the wilderness, he is accompanied by blasts of the infernal trumpet and the baying of hellhounds. Anyone unlucky enough to see this demonic sight will immediately fall to the ground stone dead. Alternatively, this crew may decide to go on a rampage, raping women in their sleep or cavorting with demonesses and witches in an orgy of carnal activity.

On quieter nights, Old Horny may decide to content himself with a hand of poker or a game of dice. For this reason, a pack of playing cards is called the Devil's Bible and a pair of dice the Devil's Bones. He may decide to catch a show at the theater (drama being one of the demonic arts) or print up some filthy tabloids to be distributed to his unwitting public. His favorite hours are noon and midnight. He is partial to dusk; but he detests dawn and will do almost anything to avoid it, perhaps it is too grisly a reminder of his old self.

When the Prince of Darkness is feeling particularly rambunctious, he will set a plague of locusts on a town or cause a shower of meteorites. He will sweep sand into harbors to bar a ship's passing and dig insurmountable ditches. He has a penchant for large feats of engineering and will spend many a night building towers, bridges, mountains, and megaliths, all of which fall down by morning. A favorite pastime is to trick happily married couples into adulterous love affairs, or to start friends and lovers quarreling.

When traveling, the Devil prefers big cities, in particular Paris, also called the antechamber to Hell, and New York City. If pushed, he will reside in any cemetery, cave, ruin, tree, mountain, grove, forest, or stream that takes his fancy.

> The Devil is not
> so black as he is
> painted.

Satyr, by Giulio Romano, 16th century

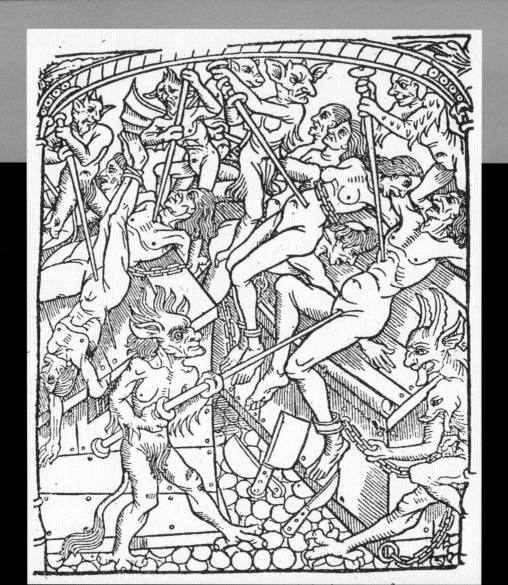

Hell and Damnation

"A terrific hell awaits the wicked—profound abyss of utter misery—
into the depths of which bad men shall fall headlong and mourn
their doom for countless years."

MAHABHARATA

A s the popular Christian story reveals, on the ninth day of his fall, Lucifer hit the ground with such velocity and weight that he sank like a cannonball straight into the earth's molten center. The surface then yawned open to suck in the rest of the falling angels. Lucifer's new abode was and is unfathomable in its unpleasantness. One can imagine the rebel angels' dismay at being cast into this cesspool of liquid fire and unbreathable air when they had once inhaled only the sweet perfume and rare atmosphere of Heaven. Lucifer was shocked by the atrocity of this final destination; but, being the cunning creature he is, he knew he must rally his crew together or face certain mutiny. Gazing out over his sooty dominion, he called his compatriots to stand before him and swore that this place, Hell (or Gehenna, or *Sheol* as the ancient Hebrews

The sin of anger is punished in Hell by dismemberment, by Nicolas Le Rouge, 1496

called it), would now be a kingdom to reckon with. Under his leadership, every divine action would be undone, every good deed matched with infamy, and every creation doomed to suffer, starting with Adam and Eve. The Devil's kingdom would be magnificent—an exact, if perverted, rival to the one they were kicked out of.

Three Realms

Hell became the bailiwick of evil where the Devil set up shop—his primary objective being to trick every living person into worshipping him as a deity and to snatch their souls when they died. The afterlife is actually divided into three realms, often referred to universally as Hell because they are all ruled by the Dark One. The pit of Hell is where sinners are sent to be punished for eternity, often receiving a specific torment that matches the grievous nature of their sin.

Limbo is the most benign of the three, a place where unblemished but unbaptized souls linger for eternity, suspended between Heaven and Hell. Limbo is the home of unchristened infants and virtuous pagan elders like Sophocles and Virgil. It is not exactly bad but not very comforting either. Its residents' punishment is the knowledge that they will never experience the joy of God's presence.

Purgatory, which appeared in writings around the twelfth century, appears to be the waiting room for the afterlife. All souls enter Purgatory and, depending on the nature of their sins, spend time there doing hard labor (like moving huge boulders from one place to another) to

Hell has three doors: lust, rage, and greed.
BHAGAVAD-GITA

redeem themselves before ascending to those pearly gates. According to the *Vision of Thurkill*, written in 1206 (see page 77), Purgatory consists of a great fire, a cold and salty lake, and a bridge covered with thorns and stakes. Each soul must pass through these trials, and the worse a sinner you are, the longer it takes. The average time one is sentenced to Purgatory is reportedly seven years, after which one's future is decided. If you have worked hard and been good, you will be given the golden ticket out; if not, depending on the judgment, you may stay in Purgatory until your next parole, or you may be sent down to the Pit. And of course, there are those souls who are so bad they bypass Purgatory altogether on the expressway to Sheol. There is no chance of redemption once you have been sentenced to burn, and, to be sure, your punishment will be in spades.

The path to heaven is depicted as being lousy with devils

History of Hell

It is an ancient and universal belief throughout many cultures that the domain of the afterlife is located somewhere beneath the earth. The word *hell* itself is associated with the old English/Germanic word for a hole in the ground or cave: *Hölle* or *Hohle*. The reasons for this common belief are myriad and varied, perhaps stemming initially from the fact that many cultures bury their dead. In Babylonia, people believed that the Sun God, in an allegory of man's journey through life, made his way across the sky every day and settled into the earth at night. Not only did this lead to the conclusion that after death one made one's home underground, but also that the center of the earth was made up of fire. Volcanic eruptions only solidified this idea. Greek and Roman mythology popularized the idea of the Underworld, ruled by the dark god Hades, or Pluto, guarded by the three-headed dog Cerberus, and accessed by crossing the murky waters of the river Styx. Every soul wound up there, regardless of its life on earth. The notion of the Underworld itself was ambiguous: the earth symbolized death, but it was also the source of life and food. Hades was not only king of the afterlife, but the god of fertility. This dynamic, in which one god and his kingdom encapsulated the potential for both life and death, fertility and sterility, prosperity and punishment was the foundation of many ancient religious traditions.

With the growth of Judaism and Christianity, the Underworld began to take on a new and terrifying status. Many cultural traditions contributed to the Christian idea of Hell, from the Apocrypha of the ancient Hebrews to Buddhist teachings of Mara, lord of darkness, to the Persian bridge of judgment. In some cultures, the otherworld was a place of punishment and horror, in others it was the final—and peaceful—resting place. In Hebrew writings, Gehenna is sixty times larger than earth and divided into seven miserable layers. As time passed, however, and Christian beliefs solidified in the European popular imagination, the vision of Hell crystallized into its present state, largely due to early and medieval writers like Saint Paul, Saint Brendan, Gregory the Great, Dante Alighieri and, later, John Milton in *Paradise Lost.*

Hades, the Greek afterlife

Landscape of the Pit

No one rendition of the landscape of Hell can be relied on since it is a rare occasion indeed that a soul has been able to descend into the Abyss, let alone return unscathed and willing to lend a description. Nevertheless, a few visionaries and saints seem to have found the Devil at home when they went calling, and their reports are bloodcurdling. A few common traits have connected the various descriptions. Most visitors to the Pit enter through the gates into a world of suffocating darkness filled with an ungodly stench and the agonized screams of sinners. As one passes through each region of Hell, progressing toward the center, the landscape grows increasingly dangerous and impenetrable, the punishments becomes more and more severe, and the howls of the damned screech louder and louder. Finally, the guest reaches the nexus of Hell, where the most egregious sinners of all are located, punished by the Evil One himself.

Dante Alighieri, the great medieval chronicler of the Inferno, writes in *The Divine Comedy* that when Lucifer struck the ground he hit in the Southern Hemisphere at the exact polar opposite of the city of Jerusalem. The earth's surface opened to swallow him, and the landmass recoiled in fear to the North—which is why the Southern Hemisphere is predominantly comprised of water. Dante also believed that the strength of the Devil's fall pushed up the mountain of Purgatory. (For his description of Hell, see page 78.) Other writers have described Gehenna as a land of unextinguishable fire and frozen plain, divided by rivers of

Judecca, an engraving of the nexus of Hell, by Gustave Doré, 19th-century engraving from Dante's Inferno

boiling blood and cliffs of razor-sharp stone. Accessed through one of three gates—one at the bottom of the sea, one in untrammeled wilderness, and one in inhabited land (some people have argued it is in Paris)—Hell's landscape encompasses icy bogs, lakes of burning pitch, valleys of thorns, and hailstorms of fire. Each region is inhabited by a native horde of demons who mete out punishments specific to that locale and to the sin associated with it.

In a departure from the eternal-fire theme, Hell has often been described by some early writers as a frozen iceberg located somewhere in the far north. This may be due in part to the inhospitable nature of the northern regions of the earth or to a fear of invading "savages" from the north. Due to this superstition, one will often find the northern side of church graveyards to be unconsecrated and reserved exclusively for the burial of suicides. In many religions, one worships facing the east, with the north on the left. The left is the traditional direction of the adversary, reflecting the Devil's original seat on the left side of God. People who are left-handed were once discriminated against due to the belief that they were kinfolk of the Devil. In Italian, *sinistre* means left.

Most descriptions of Hell claim it is a world of absolute darkness that has never been—and will never be—touched by the light of day. The only illumination comes from the light given off by the myriad torches, cauldrons, and pits of fire fueled with the souls of sinners. According to the medieval writer Furseus, there are four principal fires in Hell that will eventually consume the earth: falsehood, covetousness,

Tundal's Hell is depicted in The Inferno *by Jean Columbe, circa 1416, for the* Très Riches Heures, *a book of hours*

discord, and iniquity. The air is thick and heavy with the stench of sulfur, unbreathable by mortals. In the frozen regions, it is so cold that bones snap like twigs.

The Devil's Digs

At the center of the Inferno is the Devil's lair, a black hole of negative gravity that sucks in anything or anyone in its reach. Depending on the writer, the Devil may be bound to a gargantuan grid of hot coals, stuck waist-high in a bog, or chained in a fiery pit. In Dante's *Divine Comedy*, the three-headed Devil, or Dis, is stuck halfway in a frozen pit, grinding the traitorous bodies of Judas, Brutus, and Cassius between his teeth. Their blood and his tears of frustration mix to create a repulsive pink froth that drips from his mouth; all the while his six once-glorious wings fan the air of sin and infamy up into the mortal world. In an older Byzantine description, Satan is depicted as the awe-inspiring monarch of Gehenna, sitting on a throne of glittering diamonds with his daughters, Sin and Death, at his knee. In *Paradise Lost* Milton depicts Lucifer as a fallen warrior who, although free to move around as he pleases, slowly decays and rots, sinking into stultifying stupidity and nothingness (which is Milton's idea of Hell), dragged down by the black weight of his horrible and permanent alienation from God.

Barrators, *a vision of the bog of boiling pitch into which frauds, cheats, and barrators are plunged, by Gustave Doré, 19th-century engraving from Dante's* Inferno

He who is used to Hell is as comfortable there as anywhere else.

Government & Industry

The capitol of Hell is Pandemonium (meaning "all demons"), and it is home to the bureaucracy of evil. A huge, clanking metropolis filled with skyscrapers, pavement, and grime, Pandemonium is the ultimate urban nightmare—a direct opposite of the elysian fields and bucolic landscape in Heaven. Huge buildings house ceaseless, mind-numbing industries staffed by demons who run their business off the slave labor of the doomed. Toxic waste seeps into the earth from these factories and poisons humanity with wickedness. Earthquakes are supposedly caused by the convulsions of the damned toiling away in the bowels of the earth.

The government of Hell, in mimicry of God's dominions, is divided into seven layers, each ruled by a constituency of devils dedicated to a particular vice. (For a more specific list of who's who in Hell, see page 83.) Each constituency has a representative in the court of demons who answers to the president, the king, the ruler of Chaos—the Prince of Darkness. There is an army, a navy, and a cavalry— even an infernal orchestra. Throughout these institutions, disorder and discord run rampant—interruptions, outbursts, betrayal, sabotage—but each group keeps in mind its ultimate goal: to tempt humans to murder and mayhem and to turn them away from God.

Hell has vast resources over which to govern. Because the Devil introduced war, mechanized industry, and luxury to the world, precious ores are mined from its depths and sent up into the mortal world for

The tormented in Hell, from a German picture bible

use in weapons of war and to advance technology in an outrage of nature. Gold, silver, diamonds, and other gems are dug up and used to tempt humans with wantonness. Demons stay busy stuffing the souls of sinners into the ovens and furnaces, fueling Hell's machines and engines to keep them running smoothly. Volcanoes act as safety valves allowing the furnaces of Hell to let off steam and heat so the world doesn't blow up. According to some sources, Hell has its own publishing industry that prints up scores of blasphemous books, journals, and pamphlets to distribute above ground. Music, in particular rock and roll, is also a very lucrative business for Old Horny once you consider that he gets his payment in damned souls, not human dollars.

The Damned

Human souls make up the largest proportion of the population of Hell. Every day, more and more enter and no one ever leaves. Depending on the charge against them, prisoners of Hell may be roasted, frozen, branded with hot irons, cut with sharp knives, flogged with whips, or plunged into cauldrons of frothing acid and boiling lead. Packs of rabid dogs and rodents are unleashed to tear an unfortunate soul limb from limb. Demons with huge claws and iron beaks rip out and devour a sinner's entrails. Gargantuan beasts swallow a soul whole and slowly digest it alive, only to defecate or vomit up the remains and start the excruciating process all over again. In some cases,

The Damned in Hell (detail), by Lucca Signorelli, 17th century

7 3

sinners are parboiled and skinned alive. Because the soul is doomed to suffer eternally, no relief can be found and no one dies. Every punishment is repeated over and over again, *ad infinitum.*

The Devil does reserve special torture for certain kinds of sins, and he takes unsurpassed pleasure in punishing errant clergymen and churchgoers. For instance, people who gossip in church are sentenced to endure the ceaseless drone of their own tall tales. Holy men who fornicate have venomous serpents forced up their genitals. In an 824 account by a monk named Wetti, priests who pursued worldly goods and ignored the needs of their congregation were crucified, surrounded by a wide river of fire. Murderers, according to the twelfth-century *Vision of Saint Tunsdale*, are liquefied into a putrid broth in a searing frying pan held over a bed of hot coals. As the liquid overflows and drips down the edge of the pan like hot wax, the bodies are restored among the embers only to reignite and fuel the frying pan above. In the same tale, Saint Tunsdale writes that the greedy are devoured by a huge three-headed beast. Demons toss adulterers back and forth like a football, alternately dunking them in a frozen lake and in one filled with burning pitch.

There is a devil in every berry of the grape.

Demons carry English alewives to Hell for selling bad ale, 14th century

The Wheel of Hell diagrams the fate of the damned

Thurkill's Vision

This description of Hell summarizes Thurkill's tale, written in 1206, of a simple English laborer who is escorted to Heaven and Hell by Saint Julian. As the visitors go to the middle of the world they travel toward the east, where they approach a small church in which a flame burns brightly, fueled by the tithes of the just. In this church Saint Julian and Saint Dominus receive the souls of the recently departed and assign them their purgatorial tasks.

Just outside the church, along the northern wall, is the pit of Hell, which emanates a stench that almost strangles poor Thurkill (a sign that he has not duly tithed his crops). On the eastern side of the church, Thurkill sees the large fire of Purgatory bounded on the sides by two walls facing north and south. To the east of the walls lies an icy cold, salty lake spanned by a bridge covered with thorns and stakes. Beyond the bridge lies the Mount of Joy upon which stands a church more beautiful than one can imagine, large enough to house the entire world. Some souls must cross the purifying fire, others are immersed in the icy pond, all must traverse the bridge to get to the Mount of Joy. Depending on a soul's virtue, the journey may be swift and effortless, or it may be slow and agonizing. Prayers by the living and good deeds help speed the soul's progress.

Thurkill and Saint Julian return to the little church, where Saint Paul sits on the inside of the northern wall. The Devil stands on the outside at the flaming aperture of Hell. On the wall, between the Devil and Saint Paul, is the mighty scale they use to weigh souls. If a certain soul inclines toward the Devil, a flock of demons swoops down to hurl the sinner into the Pit. Thurkill enters Hell and is escorted to a horrific amphitheater, inhabited by row upon row of heinous demons. One miserable spirit after another is brought before the crowd to be punished for its particular vice. A vainglorious man is burned alive and torn to pieces. His dismembered limbs are then tossed in a pan and fried with pitch and fat, only to be restored whole again so another

Hell, by Taddeo di Bartolo, 1396

torture (this time inflicted by hammers and hot iron pokers) may be applied. Adulterers are forced to tear each other to shreds. Errant clergymen have their throats slit and their tongues cut off at the root. Slanderers must eat a burning spear. Murderers, thieves, arsonists, and vandals are whirled around on wheels of burning hot iron and pierced by spikes and nails. Beyond this arena of torture lies four compartments, each one containing innumerable cauldrons: the first cauldrons bubble with burning pitch; the second are filled with snow and ice; the third contain boiling sulfurous water; and the fourth feature an acidic, black liquid. Demons stand above the cauldrons poking the spirits down as they bubble up to the surface. On every eighth day, like clockwork, the demons rotate the doomed to one of the other compartments.

Dante's Inferno

Although many writers have described their vision of the city of woes, no one artist has done more to make the fires of the Inferno frighteningly real than the thirteenth-century Italian writer Dante Alighieri. In his Divine Comedy, *Dante describes "the pilgrim's" incredible journey (guided by the poet Virgil) into the afterlife of Heaven, Hell, and Purgatory, constructing a cosmology and history so detailed and precise it is hard not to believe he really was there. In fact, it has been said by those who knew him that singe marks left by the fires of Hell were clearly visible on the poet's face. Dante's rendition reads with such authority that it became the standard map of the Abyss that future writers used in their own work. Dante's Inferno is shaped like a funnel created by a series of nine rings that girdle progressively smaller spaces. One enters through the largest ring and proceeds down into the center of Hell across four rivers, descending over steep ridges, burning plains, and stony outcrops. The sins of incontinence are punished in rings one through five; the sins of violence in the seventh circle (divided into three rings); the sins of fraud in the eighth circle (called the Maleboge); and the worst sins of all, the sins of betrayal, in the ninth. The following is a brief summary.*

Outer Hell: Dante, or the pilgrim, finds himself in a dark and troubling wood on the periphery of Hell after straying from the "true path" leading up a vast, shining mountain. Lost, he encounters Virgil, who has come to guide him. They pass through the monstrous gates of Hell and are greeted with the woeful laments of those who, while alive, never took a stand for a cause or belief. They are doomed to spend eternity chasing a meaningless flag hither and thither. Those who were "never alive" in life are devoured by wasps and maggots. They cross the river Acheron on a barge piloted by Charon, the ferryman of souls in Greek mythology. The earth shakes as the barge approaches. The impure breath of evil spirits smothers the incoming souls and makes them weak.

First Circle: The pilgrim describes this as the "lip above the chasm of pain." Here they enter Limbo, where Virgil and other virtuous pre-Christian souls make their home, doomed to live without hope in an eternity of longing and knowing they will never see God. There are no cries, only deep sighs of affliction. This is the region Christ saved during the Harrowing. Great souls in Limbo, such as Homer, Plato, and Socrates, live in a separate castle with seven walls and seven gateways.

Second Circle: The travelers descend to a smaller region through a second gate. Minos, the mythological king, snarls at the entrance. As damned souls pass by him, he reviews their judgment and assigns them their place in Hell. The region is pitch black and scorched by a blustering hot whirlwind. Souls who were ruled by desire on earth are buffeted mercilessly by the unceasing gusts (Cleopatra and Helen of Troy live here).

Third Circle: Pelted by a cold and heavy rain, the travelers descend to the next circle and find the three-headed dog Cerberus, who rips the gluttons limb from limb with his talons and fangs, devouring the entrails. The souls here are mired in mud and showered with freezing hail.

Fourth Circle: Money hoarders and squanderers (those who spent their riches carelessly) are punished here, supervised by Plutus, the mythological god of wealth. The condemned souls must butt one another with enormous weights they push with their chests, griping at each other the entire time.

Fifth Circle: The pilgrim and Virgil cross the soupy marshes of the second river, the Styx, into which are thrown the envious and wrathful, who are doomed to flail endlessly at one another in frustrated anger. Beneath them, souls who spent their mortal lives in melancholy and depression lie just beneath the surface of the mud, gurgling their regrets through the muck they are fated to swallow.

Sixth Circle: On the other side of the Styx stand the burning towers that encircle the weeping city of Dis, the capital of the Inferno. Heretics moan from their tombs, arranged like catacombs outside the walls of the city. The Furies keep watch for Medusa from their perch on a tower. The visitors travel through the city on a filthy path that leads to the valley's floor.

Seventh Circle: Virgil and his guest descend through a crevice in a steep, stony ridge. They enter the first ring of the seventh circle, which is encircled by the third river, the river of blood. Those who did violence against others—arson, rape, murder, theft, and extortion—are tossed around in the river at a furious boil. The pilgrim and his guide cross the river with the help of the Centaurs and enter the Wood of Suicides, the second ring. Souls who have sinned against themselves are sent here, where they take root and grow into trees. Imprisoned within the trees, the souls bleed and break with every twig that snaps. Outside the Wood is the third ring, the great burning desert, where those who have sinned against God are pelted without mercy by a rain of fire. The third ring is bounded by the final infernal river, Phlegethon.

Eighth Circle: The pilgrim and Virgil cross the river into the Maleboge, a monstrous, teeming cesspool surrounded by steep banks and guarded by a variety of demons and giants. Here, sinners guilty of fraud are tormented. Pimps and panderers are thrown naked into a ditch and whipped by demons. Flatterers are plunged into an acidic gulf. Simoniacs (those who sell church offices) are imprisoned in holes in the wall along the banks of the pit. Only the soles of their feet show, and they are set aflame. Sorcerers and diviners have their silently weeping faces turned backwards. A bog of boiling pitch sucks in frauds, cheats, thieves, and barrators (sellers of public office). They are tormented by the Malebranche demons, who strike them with their sharp talons and beaks. Hypocrites are forced to wander the shores wearing lead mantles. Liars and their advisers are immersed in a pit of flames. Alchemists and quacks are given leprosy. Assassins and hired killers are buried face down and suffocated.

Ninth Circle: The lowest layer of Hell, the Melancholy Hole, the frozen pit of Cocytus, houses those guilty of treacherous fraud. Those who betrayed their political party or their causes are destined to cannibalize each other. Those who betrayed their guests must lie on the frozen surface of the pond weeping, their tears suffocating them as they freeze into a mask. At the center is Judecca, where the hideous body of the Devil (also called Dis) is trapped in ice. In this black hole of evil, the frothing creature perpetually gnaws on the bodies of the worst sinners of all, those who betrayed their benefactors: Judas Iscariot, Brutus, and Cassius.

O cursed sin ! O blackguardedly excess!
O treacherous homicide! O wickedness!
O gluttony that lusted on and diced
O blasphemy that took the name of Christ!
CHAUCER

Hell's Angels

Lucifer's lieutenants, Satan and Beelzebub, by Gustave Doré, 19th-century engraving

When Lucifer fell, he took with him an army of 2,400 legions of angels turned to evil. According to the sixteenth-century theoretician Johannes Wierus, there are eleven princes of Hell commanding 6,660,000 demons each, but others have estimated the numbers to be twice that. Each legion reportedly has a rebel commander who, upon entering Hell, was given a position in the Infernal Council. Like some perverted mirror of Heaven, the higher the angel's original position in Heaven the more profound the fall. In Heaven, there are nine celestial orders of angels. From the most powerful group to the least, they are: Seraphim, Cherubim, Thrones, Dominions, Virtues, Powers, Principalities, Archangels, and Angels. Each order has its own head angels or leaders who are known as princes. Lucifer appointed certain of these distinguished fallen angels to positions of authority, but luckily for humans, many principal devils have a saintly antidote in Heaven.

Although most popular legends concur that Lucifer is the Devil with a capital D, the top dog in the hierarchy of Hell, early church fathers like Saint Jerome and Cassianus promoted belief in a strict chain of command where the angel Satan was the leader. Later, Wierus wrote that the angel Beelzebub had actually usurped Satan to become the acting chief. Others (including Milton) professed that Hell is run by a triumvirate of the three. There is, as of yet, no definitive report on who is actually running the show, but it is immaterial because each rebel angel is an equally powerful arm of the octopus of evil. The following is an abbreviated list of the more well-known and significant of the fallen angels, those comrades the Devil relies on most heavily to run his kingdom who, in turn, preside over millions of lesser demons. These princes of woe spend most of their time in a state of chaotic squabbling, bickering amongst themselves, and thinking up new ways to tempt and punish humanity. (For continuity, devils are described as masculine with the understanding they can change their sex at will.)

Abbadon: The angel of the bottomless pit, also known as "the destroyer." Milton uses the name Abbadon to describe the pit of Hell. Abbadon inspires anarchy and chaos. The fallen angel of death and destruction, in Hell he is chief of the demon locusts who have the faces of humans, tails of scorpions, and bodies of winged horses. Abbadon is often associated with Satan or Sammael, and is often depicted with or confused with fellow angel of destruction, Apollyon, who holds the keys to the Abyss.

Adramelech:
The king of fire. Originally a throne angel, Adramelech is now an archdemon and a great minister of Beelzebub's Order of the Fly. When called, he manifests himself in the form of a mule or a peacock. He was overthrown by the angels Uriel and Raphael during the battle in Heaven. He is in charge of the Devil's attire and livery and is the patron of hypocrisy.

Asmodeus:
This dandified devil, the patron evil spirit behind passion, lechery, pleasure, luxury, and sensuality, runs the casinos and gambling houses in Hell. Able to appear as the most beautiful, well-dressed young man (or woman), he tempts his victims by encouraging them to buy fancy clothes and follow meaningless fads. He is the prince of profligates and loves to lure happily married couples into adulterous liaisons, sometimes with himself. This hapless devil prides himself on arranging ridiculously inappropriate marriages and leads humans into squandering their assets. He wreaks havoc in convents and monasteries by seducing the inhabitants. His mother may have been human (or, according to some, she could have been Lilith), but his father was an angel. When Asmodeus visits some poor human in his real form, he

The Devil makes his Christmas pies of lawyers' tongues and clerks' fingers.

actually has three heads symbolic of lechery, those of a bull, a ram, and a man. He also sports the feet of a rooster. He cavorts around on the back of a dragon wielding a spear. He is credited with having invented carousels, music, dancing, drama, and, one may assume, recreational drug use. Asmodeus's adversary in Heaven is John the Baptist.

Astaroth

Astaroth: The treasurer of Hell. This devil was once a seraph and now carries a viper in his hand while riding backwards on a dragon. Astaroth also serves as a diabolical coach, giving pep talks to the newer demons when they lose heart and spurring them on to greater evil. He inspires sloth and idleness. His adversary in Heaven is Bartholomew.

Azazel

Azazel: Leader of demons and related to the devil of Arabian and Islamic mythology, Iblis/Shaytan. This devil supposedly taught men how to manufacture weapons and women how to use make up. Also known as *Azael*. In his true form he has seven serpent heads, fourteen faces, and twelve wings. He may have been one of the first angels to fall for refusing to bow down before Adam and is the chief standard-bearer in Hell.

Baal

Baal: The second chief of staff of the Abyss, Baal is the patron devil of idleness. He commands sixty or seventy legions of demons and resides in the eastern region of Hell. He shows himself as a pudgy creature with the arms of a spider and three heads: a toad, a cat, and a man.

Asmodeus, the evil spirit of passion, lechery, pleasure, luxury, and sensuality, is cast out by prayer

Baal-Berith: Hell's minister of foreign affairs, chief secretary, and keeper of the infernal archives. He is often called upon to notarize pacts between humans and the Devil. A cantankerous spirit, he tempts men to be quarrelsome, contentious, and blasphemous. He also inspires them to commit murder. Baal-Berith is the patron devil of disobedience.

Beelzebub: The Devil's chief of staff and second only to Satan in the organization of Hell. Known to many as the Prince of Death, Beelzebub was Lucifer's closest companion and a fellow Seraphim angel in Heaven. Beelzebub manifests himself in the shape of a fly and presides over the Order of the Fly. He tempts men with the grandparents of all sin, envy and pride. He can send plagues of flies. Heresy is attributed to Beelzebub, who blows his bellows into the ears of heretics.

Beelzebub

Behemoth: The Devil's cupbearer, Behemoth is the patron devil of despair and gluttony. He appears in the shape of a monstrous elephant with two bear's feet. He will also take the form of a crocodile, whale, or hippopotamus and is related to Leviathan. Behemoth presides over the feasts in Hell and is responsible for dishing up food and wine for the Devil. He entertains Hell's motley crew with song and plays the role of night watchman, as he is often awake all night. Unsurprisingly, he creates chaos and havoc in the lives of men.

Behemoth

Beleth: One of the governors in Hell, Beleth presides over eighty-five legions of demons. He rides a pale horse and is announced by a blare of trumpets.

Belial/Beliar: The patron of arrogance, lies, and deceit, Belial is one of the great fallen angels. A prince of the Order of Virtues, he was created directly after Lucifer. His fall from grace was equally impressive, and he rivals Satan as a prince of darkness. The Cabalists of the fifteenth and sixteenth centuries believed him to be God's most heinous adversary. A great orator, he may appear briefly as a gentleman, but his true nature always reveals itself because the image is hollow. Belial tempts men to disloyalty, gossip, and rebellion, and instigates women to dress in finery, gossip in church, and indulge their children. In some mythologies, Belial is considered to be the original devil, a being completely separate from God and entirely evil. In this story, Belial was already actively opposing God from the bottom of the Abyss. When Lucifer fell, he joined Belial in the fiery pit and usurped his title. Belial's adversary in Heaven is Francis de Paul.

Belial

Belphegor: A party devil, Belphegor manifests himself in the shape of an attractive young woman. Once a prince of the Order of Principalities, he makes his earthly home in Paris, where he finds it easy to tempt men to licentiousness. He is the patron devil of discoveries and ingenious inventions. Belphegor is also the guardian demon of Paris—if such a thing is possible.

Carnivean: The patron devil of lewd and obscene behavior, he tempts people to act shamelessly. He is often invoked by witches during a Sabbat. His adversary in Heaven is John the Evangelist.

Carreau: Once a prince of the Order of Powers, Carreau makes people harden their hearts. His adversary in Heaven is Vincent and Vincent Ferrer.

Crocell/Procell: Another former prince of the Order of Powers, Crocell presides over forty-eight legions of evil spirits. He teaches geometry and the liberal arts and has the power to turn water freezing cold or scalding hot in moments.

Dagon: Dagon was the national god of the Philistines, appearing in the form of a kind of merman with the torso of a man and the body of a fish. He serves as the pantry chef in Hell's kitchen.

Dommiel: The patron demon of terror and trembling, Dommiel is the adversary to Saint Peter and guards the gates of Hell. (Incidentally, there are no keys for Dommiel to hold because the gates of Hell are open twenty-four hours a day and are *never* locked.)

Dumah: The Guardian of Eygpt during the Hebrew exodus, Dumah was the angel of the "silence of death." He is one of the seven princes of Hell.

> *Rake Hell and skim the devil, you can't find another such man.*

The Assyrian demon, Nirgalli

Exael: A minor devil, he was of the Order of Angels when he fell and is that much closer to humanity. Therefore, he finds it relatively easy to dwell with mortals. It was Exael who taught men how to make machines of war and to fashion jewelry from silver and gold. He may have played a role in the development of the perfume industry.

Forcas/Furcas: A senator in Hell, Forcas spends his infernal days teaching rhetoric, logic, and mathematics. He is master of the Devil's stables and can render objects invisible at will. When invoked, he can help find lost objects.

Furcalor: A murderous fallen angel once of the Order of Thrones, Furcalor enjoys sinking warships. He appears as a human with the wings of a griffin.

Gaap: Governor of the southern region of the Pit, Gaap rules sixty-six legions of demons. He manifests himself as a human sporting huge bat wings.

Gressil: Once a prince in the Order of Thrones, the lecherous Gressil now tempts men with impurity and slothfulness. His adversary in Heaven is Saint Bernard.

Haurus: One of the seventy-two devils King Solomon shut up in a brass vessel and threw into a lake, Haurus is a leader in Hell and is able to divine the truth about events occurring in the past or future. He may take the form of a leopard, a human, or some combination of both.

Hornblas: A patron devil of musical discord, he blows the trumpet to gather the ministry of Hell together.

Imamaih: Imamaih oversees voyages and can be invoked to destroy and humiliate enemies.

Kobal: The dramatist and manager of the infernal theater, Kobal tempts men with pretense and fraud.

Leviathan: The admiral of the Devil's navy, Leviathan is depicted in the Bible (Isaiah 27:1) as the primordial she- (or he-) dragon of the sea. Created with Behemoth on the fifth day, these two gargantuan devils devour damned souls. Leviathan has hordes of water demons, sprites, and nymphs to do his bidding. On Judgment Day, all but the saved will be swallowed by this sea monster.

Leviathan

Mammon: The devil of avarice, Mammon is a special ambassador to England. His supreme wickedness puts him on the same level as Satan, Beelzebub, and, in some legends, Lucifer himself. Mammon tempts men to covet belongings. He is so stooped with the weight from his fall that he cannot stand erect and spends his days staring at the ground.

Mastema: This rebel angel is the accusing angel of Hebrew mythology. He is the executioner who slaughtered the firstborn of Egypt and who tried, unsuccessfully, to murder Moses.

If the Devil be a vicar, thou wilt be his clerk.

Mephistopheles: The destroyer and the prince of deceit, Mephistopheles is a smooth character with an engaging wit and a polished manner. Due to his uniquely entertaining repartee, he is, on occasion, allowed an audience with God. Because of his dashing ways, he is often sent by the Devil to tempt modern humans to sell their souls.

Minos: Described in Canto V of Dante's *Inferno*, Minos assigns sinners to their various tortures in Hell. He has a long tail that he wraps around himself.

Misroch/Nisroch: Misroch is the Devil's cook and inspires hatred between men. He was originally an angel of the Order of Principalities and worshipped by the Assyrians. Misroch has the head of an eagle and was at one time the guardian of the famed Tree of Immortality, the fruit of which he uses in his recipes.

Nisroch

Moloch: A terrifying devil, Moloch serves as the chief of the army in Hell. He was once a Canaanite deity, worshipped by early Semites who sacrificed their firstborn children in the fires of his temple located just outside Jerusalem. Moloch's face and hands are smeared with the blood of murdered children and the tears shed by their grieving mothers.

Hell is other people.
JEAN-PAUL SARTRE

Olivier: Once an Archangel, Olivier now encourages mortals to be cruel and insensitive to the poor. His adversary in Heaven is Saint Lawrence.

Minos, by Gustave Doré, 19th-century engraving from Dante's Inferno

Paimon: A high-ranking devil, Paimon takes the form of a young woman wearing a crown and riding a camel. He is the master of ceremonies in Hell and commands two hundred legions of fiends. He supplants mortal thoughts with his own.

Rimmon: Rimmon is the only doctor in Hell. He is the ambassador to Russia and a lowly devil in the scheme of things. In Babylonian times he was believed to be the conjurer of thunder and storms. His symbol is the pomegranate.

Rofocale: Rofocale is Lucifer's second name and is synonymous with the Devil himself. In addition to being the Potentate of Evil, he has control over the world's treasury.

Rosier: The patron devil of seduction, Rosier tempts humans to fall in love. He puts syrupy words of love in the mouths of mortals and causes them to act like fools. His adversary in Heaven is Basil.

Sammael: His name is a combination of the Hebrew *sam*, meaning poison, and *el*, or angel. He is the devil of death and prince among demons and magicians. In some traditions it is he who slithers into the Garden of Eden and seduces Eve, thereby impregnating her with Cain. Sammael and Satan are often confused, and thus are interchangeable in some histories. He is reportedly a handsome, redheaded young man and is quite difficult for females to resist. Sammael is said to have a great appreciation for human art and is considered to be the first art critic.

> Hell is oneself.
> T. S. ELIOT

God and Satan vying for a man's soul as he navigates the seas of vices and sin, 15th century

Satan: Satan is the vice president of Hell, second only to the Devil himself and a significant player in the hierarchy of Hell. His name means adversary in Hebrew, and he is the angel who occupies that role in the Old Testament. One of Yahweh's angels of destruction, it is Satan who rains misfortune on the head of poor Job. In the New Testament, Satan becomes synonymous with the Devil. It is Satan who tempts Eve through the serpent and plagues Jesus in the desert. Often confused with Lucifer, Satan also was a Seraphim bedecked with twelve wings, twice the amount customarily allotted to an angel of that rank. It may be that Satan really is the Evil One, the Prince of Hell, but enough writers and artists have depicted him as Lucifer's principal vassal that he merits a separate entry here. Satan tempts humans to anger, in addition to every other sin imaginable. Satan was overthrown by the archangel Uriel.

Succor-Beloth: Another indigent devil who tempts men to lechery, Succor-Beloth presides over the Devil's harem.

Verrier: Verrier tempts men to disobey by making their necks too stiff to bow to the yoke of obedience. His adversary in Heaven is Saint Bernard.

Xaphan: A rabble-rouser of the worst sort, Xaphan suggested the rebels set fire to Heaven during the battle of angels. His idea met with a warm reception; but, before a spark could fly, the lot of them were cast into the Abyss. Xaphan fell hard thanks in part to his fiendish inventiveness. Now he fan the flames of damnation; a set of bellows is his fitting attribute.

EL DIABLITO

Satan in council, by Gustave Doré, 19th-century engraving

Raise no more devils than you can lay down.

The Watchers

In another story alluded to in Genesis and in the Book of Enoch, God created an order of seven angels called the Watchers or Grigori. They were sent to oversee the affairs of the first generations of men and to give instruction on how to survive in the distinctly un-Eden-like world outside the gates of Paradise. Once Adam and Eve began to procreate, the beauty of their daughters tempted these angels to do quite a bit more than watch. They made nightly visits, relishing the touch of human flesh. As a result, they were tossed from Heaven and landed on the surface of earth, where they espoused their mortal lovers. In the words of Genesis, "When men began to multiply on earth, and daughters were born unto them, that the Sons of God saw the daughters of men that they were fair, and they took them wives of all which they chose (6:1-2).

The Watchers are identified as the angels Armaros, Arakiel, Azazel, Baraqel, Ezekeel, Gadreel, Kawkabel, Penemue, Sarial, Samjaza, and Shamshiel.

The Watchers were giants, and they taught their human spouses the secrets of the divinity that up to then had only been whispered by God into the ears of Adam. These teachings, known as the Cabala, revealed the arts of astrology, botany, healing, and magic. But the union of these angels and women was unnatural and an outrage to God. In one legend, their progeny were born horrendous, cannibalistic monsters who ungratefully devoured their parents, and God was forced to scourge the earth to be rid of them. In another tale, the children of the Watchers were also giants, but they became great priests, poets, and artisans who taught the human race well. Regardless of the finale of these different versions, God decided to round up the Watchers and cast them into the Abyss to serve Satan. A more recent ramification of these events originated with an edict from Saint Paul, who demanded in the New Testament that women be veiled in church to avoid tempting the angels, lest the Holy Father lose any more of his Cherubim.

Lilith

Although Lilith was not an angel, she was directly created by God. The Devil's consort, the Queen of Hell, and the daughter of night, Lilith is a holy terror. Driven by an insatiable hunger of envy, Lilith stalks the world by night raping men in their sleep and sucking their blood, or stealing newborn children from their cribs and eating them. According to ancient Hebrew beliefs, God created Lilith to be Adam's first wife; but he made them equal, connected back-to-back like Siamese twins. When they argued incessantly, God decided to split them into individual people, but this did not do. Lilith hated being a housewife under her husband's thumb all the time. She questioned masculine supremacy and was not a big fan of the missionary position, which was what Adam (and, one surmises, God) preferred in their sexual relations.

Lilith ran away with a band of demons, with whom she spawned a generation of evil creatures called Lilin or Lilis, often depicted as owls. Owls were considered to be evil birds of night that

could not look directly at light. As bad as she was, Adam missed her and complained of his loneliness to his maker. God created Eve (from Adam's rib, lest there be any lingering question who was dominant) and sent three angels—Sanvi, Sansanvi, and Semangalef—to fetch Lilith. They found her with her vile progeny and demanded she return, but she would not. As punishment, God decreed she be banished and that all of her children die in infancy. Lilith grew despondent and went to throw herself in the Red Sea. The three angels were genuinely moved by Lilith's despair and compensated her with power over newborn boys for the first eight days of their lives, the first twenty days for newborn girls. Lilith in return promised not to harm children who had the three angels' names written anywhere near them.

Alone outside of Paradise, Lilith happened upon another creature divorced from God, the Devil, who in the Talmud legend takes the name of Sammael. Bound by their mutual hatred of humanity, Sammael and Lilith spawned a generation of devils and wicked creatures. Some beliefs claim it was Sammael and Lilith who plotted the downfall of mankind in Eden. In many artistic representations, the serpent is actually Lilith, not Satan. In others, Satan seduces Eve while Lilith works her charm on Adam, and it is all euphemized in the idea of tasting forbidden fruit. While many cultures revile Lilith as the epitome of evil femininity, in others she has come to represent the fight for women's equality and free sensuality. In the Talmud, it is not Lilith's hatred for babies that drives her into nurseries, but her love of them. Barren for eternity, she longs to press a warm baby against her breast. According to the same belief, if a baby smiles during the Sabbath, Lilith is amusing it.

*Lilith, the Queen of Hell
and the daughter of night*

The Hordes of Hell

As numerous as the princes of Hell are, they require legions of demons to do the Devil's work. Like venom from the fangs of a snake, wave upon wave of diabolical creatures spew from the maws of the Abyss to live among humankind, ready at will to execute any nefarious order commanded by their leader. And they keep coming. As more humans die, the souls of the damned descend into the belly of the earth to spawn new demons, temptations, and sins for the good people of the earth to resist. Demons differ from devils in that demons originated as natural, familiar spirits, both good and bad, who were worshipped in pagan religions. Their name comes from the Greek word *daimon*, which means spirit. Demons cause disturbances of a physical nature, like storms, illness, and earthquakes. Devils, on the other hand, are

Last Judgement (detail), by Giotto di Bondone, Scrovegni Chapel, Padua

1 0 5

associated with moral depravity and sin. The word *devil* comes from the Greek *diabolos,* meaning perjurer or slanderer, and it has always defined a singularly evil spirit. Demons differ from devils in that they were never angels; they were not created directly by God, nor have they inhabited Heaven or been in the presence of the Lord. Because demons were evil from the moment of their conception, they never fell from grace into the Abyss and, consequently, are free to roam around earth, coming and going from Hell as they please. The numbers vary, but it is certain that as long as humans continue to do bad things, new demons hatch every day. The Talmud quotes that there are 7,405,926 hosts of evil, but more recently the theologian Martinus Barrhaus tabulated 2,665,866,746,664. When Saint Macarius of Alexandria prayed to God that he might be able to see what evil spirits lurked among men, God opened his eyes and the demons swarming in the air around him were "as numerous as bees."

The only purpose evil spirits have is to tempt human beings while they are alive and torment their souls in Hell when they die. Because demons, for the most part, cohabit with humanity above ground, they have wormed their way into popular culture and can be blamed for anything from a run of bad luck to losing one's keys to the most malicious sin and devastating disease. According to Norse tradition, the great tree of life, Yggdrasil, had roots that dug deep into the Underworld, and it was suspected that demons sprouted from its subterranean branches. From pagan beliefs in natural deities to modern

The Last Judgment (detail), by Hieronymous Bosch, circa 1500

fears of vampires and ghosts, the idea of deviltry has evolved through the ages into widespread superstitions that have persisted despite efforts by organized religions to dispel them. Regardless of religion or country, most cultures resound with tales of bone-chilling brushes with spirits that may take the form, among others, of fairies, ghosts, elves, or monsters.

Although certain tribes of these spirits may be misunderstood and many might help instead of hinder a person (especially if bribed or complimented), they are all grouped here under the demonic umbrella because of their associations with the natural world, supernatural phenomena, and the Devil rather than with God and the spirit. Their goals may be the same as the rebel angels, but demons are of the earth, they were never heavenly bodies, and thus they fall lower on the diabolical totem pole.

Demonic Characteristics

Demons from Hell reek with an ungodly stench. Rotten to the core, plebian devils eat and vomit excrement and possess people to make them do the same. Most powerful at the witching hour—noon and midnight—the Devil's servants cavort in the air around us, shake the earth we walk on, and agitate the water we bathe in. Ready to invade a body through any orifice, demons lurk around humans waiting for them to slip up—to gossip in church, forget their prayers, stuff their bellies, or lust after their neighbor's wife.

The jaws of Hell with Lucifer (above) and Satan (below)

The demons and spirits of hell, 15th century

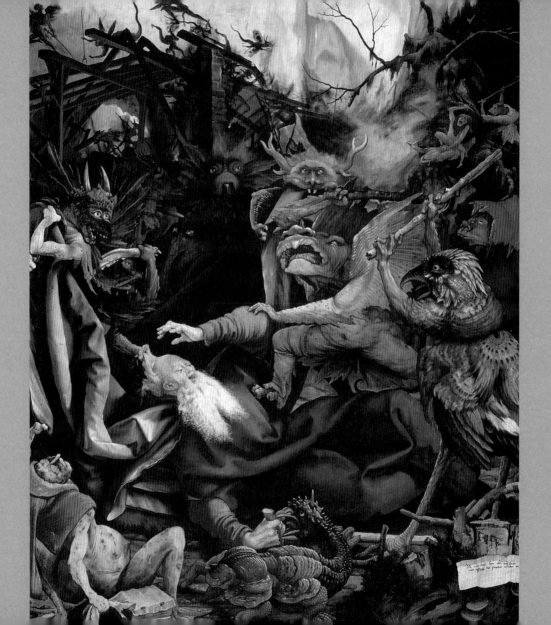

They like to sit under bridges and at crossroads and tempt travelers. Not content to let us fail in our own right, they lay irresistible temptations across our path, leading us down the road to damnation with the skip and whistle of good intentions. Demons cause pestilence and disease; they stir up storms and shipwrecks. They can trick us into heeding their words by simulating a loved one's voice. The murderous ones will throw stones, hurl victims off precipices, and make others drive into trees. If one resists, they may bring on a scourge of fleas, ticks, lice, skin rashes, or insomnia in hopes of coercing their victim into submission.

Demons, contrary to popular belief, are attracted to churches and clergymen; they experience exquisite delight when tormenting the holy. The desert saints (ascetic believers who renounced the world to live as devout hermits in the desert) were especially prone to bewitchment and had to be on guard at all times. Saint Anthony, one of the more famous desert fathers, was continously beset upon by demons while he went about his affairs. They harassed and tempted him in the form of vicious animals and, on occasion, beautiful women. Because unclean spirits flock to holy ground, churches and other religious places must be fully exorcised before any services are permitted. When demons are expelled from a church during its consecration, they scurry up the walls and out onto the roof. From this perch, they harass people entering the building; thus the preponderance of gargoyles on the roofs of state and holy structures.

The Temptation of St. Anthony, by Mathias Grünewald (from the Isenheim Altarpiece), 16th century

111

The Family Tree

Demons exist in every crack and crevice of the globe. In Japan they are called *oni;* in India, *devas;* in England, *bogies;* and in Scotland, *gyres;* but by any name, fiendish spirits are up to no good. Demonologists throughout the ages have tried to sort out a hierarchy of demons, leaving a morass of definitions in their wake. It is generally agreed that, although certain similarities exist, we pitiful humans have no way of knowing whether we are dealing with a good spirit or an evil one. To be on the safe side, one should expect the worst. According to Guazzo's *Compendium Maleficarum* (1608), there are six families, or genera, of demons:

Fiery: The first are demons who dwell in the upper air and will not touch ground or cause trouble until the Last Judgment.

Aerial: The second are devils who stir up the atmosphere and cause turbulence, storms, hurricanes, and thundering tempests as they try to destroy mankind. These creatures may descend into Hell and will make themselves visible to humans if called upon to do so.

Terrestrial: Living in forests, glens, and knolls, these hellions lay in wait for unsuspecting passersby. One is apt to find them in a lonely field or behind a rocky outpost giving false directions to lost travelers. Of all the families, these demons are the most common; they live secretly among people, mimicking their habits and befriending them in order to learn their darkest secrets and betray them.

When the Devil prays, he has booty in his eye.

Reformation-era vision of the mouth of Hell

Aqueous: Living in oceans, rivers, and streams, these powers of darkness raise storms at sea, sink ships, and drown swimmers. Associated with mermaids and the sirens from the *Iliad,* they frequently appear in seductive female forms. Their leader is the ignominous beast Leviathan (see page 93).

Subterranean: This batch of demons lives in caves and caverns and harasses miners and other workers who toil beneath the earth. They are the source of earthquakes, wildfire, and dry, hot winds that scourge the earth.

Heliophobic: The final breed of demons are the most malicious. Homicidal and merciless, these demons only appear at night and, with one blast of their noxious, icy breath, will kill a person who has the misfortune of running into them.

Within these families of demons are subcreatures who have populated bad dreams and haunted human beings for centuries, some of which serve a specific purpose. Heathen activities such as dancing, blasphemy, promiscuity, miserliness, tyranny, laziness, gambling, and pride all have their patron demons. Diseases like asthma, croup, insanity, and indigestion are also caused by particular devils, as are phobias of heights, water, and flying. In fact, almost every blight on the face of the earth can be attributed to some sort of evil spirit of the same name. Of the millions of demons, a few stand out in their foul ignominy.

The devil argues his case, from the Dictionaire Infernal

Ahrimanes: In a Persian tale that influenced development of the Christian idea of evil, the Ahrimanes are angels that followed their leader, Ahriman, to stage a revolt against the principle of good, known as Orzud or Ormazd. Ahriman and his followers were expelled and went to live on earth, where they were rejected. As revenge, Ahrimanes injure the earth's inhabitants. They now live in the space between the stars and the earth.

Beast 666: According to the book of Revelation, the end of the world will be heralded by the unleashing of a horrible demon into the world. In one final, desperate attempt to reassert himself, the Devil will send a false prophet—the Antichrist—and the Beast 666, a ferocious apocalyptic creature who rises from the sea ridden by the whore of Babylon. Beast 666 is a scarlet-hued monstrosity with the body of a leopard, the feet of a bear, and the jaws of a lion. It sports ten horns and seven heads, and spews blasphemy and haughty words from each of its seven mouths. It will have power over the world for forty-two months, and within that time "dwellers on earth whose names have not been written in the book of life from the foundation of the world will marvel to behold the beast, because it was and is not and is to come." (Revelation 17:8). The Beast will lay waste to all around it, visiting plague and destruction on the lives of mankind and defeating the power of the saints. In time, the Beast will be accompanied by the false prophet, or Antichrist, who will trick people into believing that

Last Judgment, by van der Heyden, engraving from a drawing by Peter Bruegel the Elder, 1558

he is the Messiah. The Antichrist will fashion brazen images of the Beast, commanding the masses to adore it. He and the Beast will brand their followers with the mark 666 upon their forehead or hand, and anyone who resists will be slaughtered. According to the prophecy, the Day of Reckoning will dawn in a place called Armageddon; the false prophet, Beast 666, and the legions of evil will do battle with the Son of God, seated "faithful and true" upon his dazzling white horse, and an army from heaven bedecked in gleaming white linen. In the long-awaited final triumph of good over evil, Judgment Day will come and the false prophet and Beast 666 will be captured and hurled into a boiling lake of fire and brimstone. The Devil will be chained and locked in Hell for a term of a thousand years, and all true believers who refused to succumb to the Beast will be saved.

Assyrian goat demons

Djinns: Also known as jinns or genii, some of these Arabian spirits are good and others are bad. The evil ones enter the body through all five orifices, going straight for the head to drive their victim mad. The good ones can be persuaded to grant favors and wishes. They are related to another band of Persian monstrosities, the *div*. The djinns' tendency to enter a human through the mouth or nose has led to the precaution of covering one's mouth when yawning or coughing and saying "*Gesundheit*" or "God Bless You" when another sneezes.

Elves: Related to and often confused with fairies and goblins (see pages 119, 121), elves are created from the root of the magical mandrake plant. If treated well, they can be wonderful helpmates, amassing great wealth and power for their master. If treated cruelly, an elf will see that its owner gets his or her just desserts—often in a violently grotesque fashion. Occasionally, elves collaborate with witches, especially in swapping one of their own children, otherwise known as changelings, with newborn human infants. Hopdance is a famous Scottish elf who goads people into frenzied dancing and orgiastic frivolity.

Fairies: Known in different parts of the world as nymphs, little people, trolls, or sprites, these creatures play a vital role in popular superstition. Their origins are most likely pagan, and thus they have been demonized by organized religions. As a group, they are usually diminutive and capricious, as likely to lend a hand as they are to torment and tease. For the most part, these entities live in the natural places they protect: trees, fields, forests, rivers, banks, bridges, and stony ledges, for example. They are easily whipped into a fury if proper respect is not paid to their home, but their wrath can be avoided with gifts of food, flowers, or coins. They adore lovers, music, dance, and laughter, but once crossed can be vicious enemies. They are often responsible when something is missing, as they look at any human possession as fair game. The more malicious kinds will kill or maim a human, but only if the person stupidly blunders into their territory without heeding their rules or paving the way with a small gift. They can be warded off with iron or steel since they abhor any element of

> *Hell is full of good meanings and best wishings.*
> GEORGE HERBERT

Knockers frighten a miner

industry or violence. According to some, these little people are actually fallen angels who were saved from Hell by Christ. As the angels fell, Christ lifted his hand to stop the least responsible beings at the earth's surface, thus some vestige of goodness has remained in them.

Fates: These three hags are memorialized in Homer's *Odyssey*. One spins the yarn of a person's life, one measures its length, and the last snips it off with her sharp shears. The demonologist Alphonsus de Spina believed the fates were not real women but demons.

Ghouls: Also known as ghosts, ghouls tend to haunt graveyards and unearth the freshly buried. In some Middle Eastern cultures, ghouls were thought to devour small children and corpses. These undead creatures also like dark lonely places such as mountain tops and windswept plains. Legend has it that dogs can see ghouls, which is why they occasionally bark at what appears to be nothing to the human eye. If you want to see a ghoul, stand behind a dog and look between its two ears down the middle of its head.

Gremlins: Generally good-natured, gremlins usually behave badly when they are pulling pranks. Gremlins are goblins that haunt the air, traumatizing pilots and air travelers by suddenly swooping up from their underground pits around airports and landing strips and grabbing a plane's wing. They are green in color and covered with mossy hair, and they use their webbed feet to suction onto airplanes and other industrial machines. They empty full fuel tanks, disorient the gauges in the cockpit, and cause turbulence. An old wives' tale claims that when you hear thunder, the rumbling comes from the gremlins' favorite pastime, sky bowling. As technology advances, gremlins have found new arenas in which to play their tricks; computers, telephones, and televisions are only a few of the modern machines they now haunt.

Harpies: The Harpies are hags from Hell, vicious shrews repulsive to behold. They torment their victim with unearthly screeches and wails, all the while scratching eyes out and tearing flesh with their hideously long fingernails. Ladies of the night, Harpies may initially take the form of beautiful women to seduce their victims into lustfulness; but inevitably, as passions mount, they will suddenly reveal themselves, more often than not causing the death of their victim. The wailing banshee that visits an Irish family to announce an impending death is a commonly seen Harpie.

Hellhound: The three-headed guard dog of the gates of Hell, the hellhound is related to the Roman dog Cerberus who stood at the entrance to Hades. The dog's heads are a parody of the Holy Trinity. The hellhound accompanies the Devil on his night hunts.

Demon

> *Were it not for gold and women there would be no damnation.*
> CYRIL TOURNEUR

121

Hobgoblins or Goblins: Related to fairies and other little devils, goblins, or cobolds, are predominant in England and Ireland. Rarely seen in cities, goblins are sooty-faced, hirsute creatures who loiter around rural villages and farmhouses causing trouble for the folks they live with. Blowing out hearth fires, knotting up ropes, and undoing chores are only a few examples of the pesky tricks these demons play. Their acts are hardly ever fatal, and if they happen to be in the mood, goblins will occasionally complete a task left undone.

Imps or Familiars: Imps take the form of small animals, rodents, insects, or frog-like creatures. They are the errand-boys of witches, who send them off to execute a particular spell or charm. Because they are small, they are easily kept in boxes, bottles, or pockets. Witches suckle them on a third teat, otherwise known as the Devils' Mark (see page 143).

Incubi: An incubus, meaning "to lie on," is one of a horde of demons who take human shape and descend on sleeping women in the middle of the night, either raping them or inspiring lustful dreams and desires. Nuns and maidens are often the victims of the incubus's visit, and a pregnancy in a convent is usually the result of such a visit. Copulation with an incubus, reports claim, is a decidedly disgusting affair. The entity allegedly sports an immense frozen penis that he uses to tear viciously into the internal organs of his victims. If, as unbelievable as it may seem, a woman invites an incubus to her bed, all members in the household will fall into a trancelike sleep, even the woman's mortal

Demons torment the damned in the right panel of The Last Judgment, *by Hans Memling, 15th century*

lover who may be snoring alongside her. In the Middle Ages, any baby born with a mental or physical deformity was considered to be the progeny of this vile union.

Knockers: Knockers are yet another tribe of little people who torment miners working underground in tunnels and caves. If a worker happens to catch sight of a Knocker or approach one, legend has it that he will come down with painful rheumatism. If left alone, Knockers are generally considered harmless.

Luciferge: These hideous demons roam the earth searching for souls to kidnap and bring down to Hell. Equipped with razor-sharp talons and beaks they use to tear the soul from its body, they are the henchmen that come to collect on a deal made with the Devil. Their counterparts, the Malebranche, torment some of the worst sinners in Hell. These unnatural beasts have snakes coming out of their noses and ears and sport cloven hooves and tails like their beloved leader. When a doomed individual takes his last breath, the Malebranche leap on his soul with whoops of joy and carry it off to its horrible fate in a cloud of stinking, sulfurous smoke. Mourners present at the moment of death have been known to catch a whiff of the telltale odor of damnation.

Nightmare or Mares: Waking with shortness of breath or a heaviness in the chest is evidence of a visit by a nightmare demon.

Demon of the Medieval Danegelt tax on wine

These heinous creatures attack at night, sitting on a person's chest and breathing putrid breath into their nostrils. Their exhaust causes horrible dreams; and if the person awakes while the demon is still present, he or she will be paralyzed under the weight of the monster.

Poltergeists:

Also called "jumping demons," these creatures reside in people's homes and play irritating tricks at night. They will break dishes, hide belongings, shake the walls, and turn lights and stereos off and on. Poltergeists like to creep up and rip the covers off sleeping victims. They also love to stand at the edge of the bed and tickle the bottoms of feet. Occasionally a poltergeist gets violent, resulting in injury to their victims or, more rarely, death. For the most part, however, poltergeists are harmless, albeit irksome and often terrifying household pests.

Succubi:

The female counterpart to the incubus, a succubus (meaning "to lie under") attacks innocent men in their sleep. The denizens of Lilith, succubi sit astride a man's prone body and have their way with him. Often taking the form of beautiful women, succubi will instantly turn into miserable hags if confronted with their real identities. Monks in monasteries are often visited by these troublesome spirits who inspire dirty dreams and tempt the brethren with their lusty ideas. In the Middle Ages, fearful monks tied crucifixes to their genitals before retiring at night as protection against nocturnal visits by succubi.

A Greek demon called Zrvan Akarana

The Devil is subtle yet weaves a coarse web.

Monsters

The following entities cannot technically be called demonic as they are not sent by the Devil to tempt and torment the innocent, nor do they play a role in punishing sinners in Hell. However, being a foul and notorious group, they perpetrate violence and evil on the world and call upon dark forces for their powers. For this reason, they are included here.

Vampire

Vampires: A ruthless group of undead who surface only at night to suck the blood of the living. Once mortal, these corpses were raised from the dead and granted eternal life by the forces of evil; the catch is they must drink fresh, warm blood in order to survive. Virtually helpless during the day—sunlight is fatal—vampires sleep the sleep of the dead in hidden lairs, either in deep caves or in locked coffins, until sunset. They have the ability to transform themselves into many forms—bats, rats, wolves, shadows, even a sinister, creeping fog. Annals of vampiric legend and lore have been collected throughout the ages, and there have been many eyewitness accounts of their existence. Many rules and advisories have evolved about how to behave when confronted with a vampire— garlic, holy water, and the sign of the cross seem to ward them off—but the only *sure* way to do away with one of these ghastly beings is to find its lair by day, drive a wooden stake through its heart, and chop off its head. In what could be called vampiric tradition, certain Black Masses reportedly profane the Eucharist by celebrating a ceremony in which worshippers drink human blood from a gold vessel.

Werewolves: Lumped in the same category as vampires due to their ability to change shape, their nighttime proclivity, and their fondness for human flesh, werewolves are half-human, half-wolf creatures that have a penchant for juicy young maidens and farmers' livestock. They are especially powerful during full moons and occasionally stalk their victims in packs. In some traditions, one can become a werewolf by petitioning the Devil. In others, those bitten by a werewolf will metamorphose into one too. Werewolves return to their human form at dawn, so it is impossible for most normal folks to know who is one and who isn't.

Zombies: Living corpses who find their origin in West Indian, Caribbean, and Voodoo legend, zombies are used by evil-doers as servants. The zombie is actually a poor soul that, having just been buried, is unable to move peacefully into the afterlife because it is called forth by someone on earth. Once it answers, the zombie climbs out of its freshly dug grave to heed its master's call, obeying whatever commands the master makes. With human nature being what it is, these orders are usually wicked. To ensure that their loved ones get safely into the afterlife, many West Indian cultures bury their dead face down, with their mouths full of dirt and their lips sewn shut.

Asian Demons

It is difficult to give a brief overview of some of the darker deities that populate Asian mythology without outlining the basic tenets of Buddhism, Brahmanism, Confucianism, Taosim, Hinduism, Khmer, and Shinto—a process that would take another book. These religions have evolved over thousands of years into an intricate, often cross-woven, web of belief incorporating many different kinds of evil, sin, and punishment. Perhaps the most striking contrast between these religions and those of the West is their faith in reincarnation. Consequently, their notions of Hell reflect the idea that a soul is punished in the netherworld to excoriate sins committed in a former life, the success of which determines the condition that the soul will be reborn to.

China: Among the many demons that have evolved from the hybridization of Buddhism, Taoism, and Confucianism in China, *Gosirsa* (Ox-Head) and *Asvamukha* (Horse-Face) are two to

 be avoided. They are the souls of men who, while alive, either ate beef or mistreated horses. They descend upon a soul at death and snatch it away to the Ten Hells. Each hell has its respective king who metes out a specific torture appropriate to the sin. The kings serve under the deity Yama. Taoist monks have the power to fend off demons.

Japan: The *oni* are "deities that cause disaster," and during the Heian period in Japan (782-897 A.D.) belief in them grew very strong. There are two kinds of *oni*, those that inhabit the nether regions and those that live among mortals on earth. The former are especially fearsome, with bodies colored either red or green and sporting the head of an ox or a horse. They whisk sinners away to Hell, or *Jigoku*, in their fiery chariots. The supreme judge in Hell, which consists of eight hot hells and eight frozen hells, is Emma-Ô, who records all the sins of the departed in his book. Certain individual *oni* are blamed for specific diseases, starvation, cruelty, and disfigurement.

Tibetan demon

Cambodia: The spirits of Khmer mythology are evil-looking creatures with distended bellies, emaciated limbs, and the faces of pigs called *pretas* or *kmoch.* These demons eat excrement, vomit fire, and tear at their own flesh. A *preta* can appear in the form of a wild animal. A group of subdemons, the *kmochpray,* are the souls of women or children who died in childbirth. These ghouls will storm the body of a near relative, causing suffering and death. Occasionally demons can be bribed with offerings.

Persia: In addition to the *jinn* and the *div, ghuls* and *ifrits* are the most common and dangerous Persian demons, able to adopt the shape of a loved one in order to lure their victims to an isolated spot and devour them. *Nasnas* is a vicious sea monster masquerading as a helpless old man who waits at the banks of rivers, asking passersby to help him across. When one does, the fiend drops his helpless façade and drowns his poor benefactor. *Palis,* or foot-licker, attacks wanderers in the desert by licking the soles of their feet until he has sucked their blood dry.

Japanese Oni *headed for* Jigoku

"Double, double, toil, and trouble,
Fire burn and cauldron bubble.
Cool it with a baboon's blood
Then the charm is firm and good."
SHAKESPEARE,
THE WITCHES' CHANT FROM *MACBETH*

Handmaidens of the Devil

But what about the *mortal* legions of evil? Those *humans* who have sworn their allegiance to the Prince of Darkness to advocate his cause and attract increasingly more people into his diabolical fold? Of all the admirers of the Devil, the most renowned and persecuted group in history is witches. The sisterhood of Devil's brides, wielding dark powers and uncanny knowledge, serves the Archfoe in his mission to dominate the world. Although there are "white" witches who reportedly perform good magic, most handmaidens of the Devil are bent on mayhem and destruction. They curse their enemies, poison livestock, steal children, and ruin fortunes. Those who practice witchcraft are predominantly female. Male witches, or warlocks, have been identified, but they are an afterthought, mere mascots of Hell's sorority of sin. (For male practitioners of the

Witches Sabbath
by Francisco Goya,
circa 1800

black arts, see Sorcerers, page 149). Witches band together in protective groups of thirteen, also called covens, and the covens periodically convene in a ritual gathering called a Sabbat. Nevermind that most "witches" brought to trial during the sixteenth and seventeenth centuries were widowed, middle-aged, or elderly women with property and no heirs, which meant their inheritance would go to the government if they were found guilty. Or that women once revered for their healing arts were burned at the stake for competing with doctors. It was common knowledge at that time that women were one bat of an eyelash away from depravity anyway; all it took was a nod from Satan and a taste of his deviant ways for the "weaker vessel" to become his slave.

Witch's Work: According to the inquisitors of the fif-

teenth, sixteenth, and seventeenth centuries, witchcraft had one primary objective: to increase the Devil's power over humanity and seduce ever-increasing numbers of people into his fold. Before that, witches were accepted—if feared—denizens to be consulted for every imaginable human dilemma, from curing warts to attracting lovers to making fields fertile the following spring. Witches, however, were not granted immense powers by their master. Kept in a state of perpetual bondage to the Devil, a witch must perpetrate a certain amount of wrongdoing to maintain his favor. If pleased, the Fiend would tutor a witch in more advanced forms of treachery and shower her with gifts and gold. The witch must constantly renew

The Witch of Endor
conjures the spirit of
Samuel for King Saul

her pact with Satan, proving her love for him in circumscribed rituals of worship (see Sabbat, page 136).

Powers of Witches:
A witch's power, though limited, could be dangerous, even fatal. It was widely accepted that if a loved one fell mysteriously ill or had fits of hysteria, a witch was most likely the cause. Children and animals are especially susceptible to the Evil Eye, whereby a witch will blight them with one glance. Once crossed, a witch makes a formidable enemy. Crops will shrivel, livestock will fall stone dead in the fields, or festering sores will erupt on flesh; it is not uncommon for people afflicted by a witch's curse to perish eventually. A witch can be far away and still cast her spells. She can instantaneously make herself invisible or change into a rabbit, toad, or mouse. Her companion in iniquity, her familiar, is at her beck and call and often performs the dirty deeds for her. The worst part is one can never tell if one is dealing with a witch, as they appear exceedingly normal, if a mite contentious, by day. By night, however, a witch's power grows manifold and one needs precautions if venturing out alone.

Serpent before the curse

A Witch's Tools:
A witch is most powerful at night, especially on full moons. She has an arsenal of lethal concoctions derived from varied mixtures of bodily fluids, exotic animal parts, and herbs. She may or may not have secret potions and oils given to her by Satan. Using a hand cut from a dead man to hold her candle

(otherwise known as a Hand of Glory), a witch can enter any room without waking the sleeping inhabitants. Using wax effigies or nail parings, locks of hair, or eyelashes stolen from her victim, she can wreak a painful vengeance or cast a destructive spell. Witches record their incantations, spells, and charms in books of black magic called *grimoires*. Recipes for how to make a Hand of Glory (it must be pickled in an earthenware jar for two weeks with salt, saltpeter, and peppers), turn oneself into a frog, and inflict leprosy are only a few of the skills taught in these workbooks.

Conjuring the Devil

The Devil never sent a wind out of Hell but he would sail with it.

Sabbat: The Sabbat is a grand gathering of covens brought together to worship the Devil. A prescribed ritual, the Sabbat is where the Evil One communes with his brides and bestows on them their menacing power. This meeting usually takes place in an isolated spot, protected from nosy snoops. The most significant Sabbat occurs on Walpurgis Night (April 30th), also called Toodmas in England. Interestingly, this same date was revered by pagans as the beginning of spring—the season of fertility; the same celebration is also the origin of May Day. Other Sabbats occur on Halloween (October 31), Candlemas (February 2), and Lammas (August 1). Covens have local meetings every month during the full moon and worship weekly on Thursday nights. The preparation for the Sabbat is a sacred activity and one witnessed by few mortals who have lived to describe it.

Witches are so good at hiding their identity, they can be married and have a family that is completely unaware of their ghastly powers. By day she may be a doting wife and mother; but as the moon rises, her true identity reveals itself. On the night of the Sabbat, the witch casts a spell of drowsiness on her brood; once they are asleep she creeps from her bed and strips off her clothing. She imbibes a magic oil and annoints herself with three drops of a sacred unguent given to her by Satan. As she goes through this ritual, her normal countenance falls away to reveal her true face—a hideous, lecherous mask—and her body transforms into a reflection of death. Standing defiantly astride a piece of wood as small as a twig, she swoops up the chimney or out the window

The witches' Sabbat

and flies off to a deserted glen or guarded mountain top.

There she congregates with her fellow witches, warlocks, and a flock of demons to wait for their king. As the Prince of Evil approaches, often in the form of a goat with a huge erect phallus (resembling the Roman god of fertility, Priapus), the witches gleefully surround him shouting their devotion. Each worshipper plants a kiss on his hairy backside and the meeting is called to order. A Black Mass, a profane version of the Eucharist, is conducted in which the witches and demons recite the liturgy backwards—or simply recite "Beelzebub, Beelzebub" over and over—and chew on a black host, followed by buckets of strong wine. To further prove their abhorrence of faith, they may trample a cross, shout profanities at the Lord, or blaspheme the saints. Occasionally a live sacrifice of an animal or a newborn child is offered. Once that is completed, business affairs are dealt with. New members are inducted. Veteran witches are called upon to relate what misdeeds they have perpetrated since the last Sabbat. If their activities are bad enough to please the Devil, he gives them a gift. If they have not fulfilled their quota, demons hang them by their arms in midair. The new witches are presented with their familiars.

At the close of business, the entire group falls to uproarious drinking and feasting. The fare is more often than not some gruesome vittle such as the entrails of a hanged man. After gorging themselves, the witches and demons rise to dance holding hands in a circle. The music is discordant and obscene, played on grotesque instruments

Witches conjuring
up a hailstorm,
15th century

139

fashioned from skulls and bones. The dancers whirl around faster and faster, spinning and chanting until their frolic degenerates into orgiastic frenzy. Cavorting, fornicating, and sodomizing each other with abandon, the witches do not leave until each and every one has consummated its love with the Devil himself—a questionable treat, considering the report that the Devil's genitals are shaped like gargantuan, spiked forks and are cold as ice. The witches eventually collapse from exhaustion and are whisked away on their broomsticks in time to be home before dawn. As the sun begins its ascent, all traces of the Sabbat disappear but for a subtle scent of sulfur and singed flesh that hangs in the air.

Hunting Witches:

The Devil's rewards for service must have been sizeable, for it appears that by the sixteenth century almost every town or rural outpost had a local "witch." During the witch-hunt craze of the seventeenth century, tens of *thousands* of witches were executed by their fellow townspeople in Europe and America. Thoroughly convinced of their righteousness, accusers maintained that a witch was filled with an insatiable, incurable lust for evil and vicious deceit. She was cunning, immoral, and depraved and, what's worse, not content to keep it to herself. Witches had supernatural powers of seduction and would lure an unwary soul into forfeiting its virtue. The *Malleus Maleficarum* is a large, rather astonishingly detailed volume of confessions put together by two German inquisitors under the papal bull against witchcraft in 1484. If there could be any lingering doubt,

Woman of abomination, by Albrecht Dürer, 15th century

141

the publication of this book proved to most that the witch drew her destructive power directly from the iniquitous fires of Hell, the belly of Beelzebub, and everyone was better off if she were dead.

Witches were identified in a number of ways during the witch-hunts. A woman accused of witchcraft would be brought before a crowd, stripped, and completely shaved to see if she sported the Devil's Mark or Seal. Almost any blemish could be called a Devil's Mark, but the inquisitors looked initally for a large birthmark or scar that resembled a cloven hoof. If found, the inquisitor would take a large needle and prick it deeply into the mark. If the prick did not hurt or draw blood, it was taken as a true sign that the woman had been chosen to serve in the legions of doom. If no blemish was found, the accused was probed for the presence of a Witch's Teat. Any protuberance on the flesh, even a mole or wart, could presumably be a third teat the witch used to suckle her familiar. A person who traveled in the company of a small animal or rodent was in constant danger of being thought a witch, since familiars often took the form of mice, rats, cats, or dogs. Another surefire way to catch a witch was to immerse her in water with her left thumb tied to her right foot, a process called "swimming the witch." If she floated, her wickedness was proven because the pure water would not "accept" her; if she sank she was declared innocent but, as was often the case, drowned.

Implements used to torture witches, 16th century

"Wherever God erects a house of prayer,
The Devil always builds a chapel there;
And 'twill be found upon examination,
The latter has the largest congregation."

DANIEL DEFOE

Running with the Devil

"Set out running but I'm takin' my time
A friend of the Devil is a friend of mine."

ROBERT HUNTER

Witches are not the only mortals inhabiting the shadowy world of black magic and Devil worship. In fact, Satan has found no lack of acquaintances above ground, despite the tragic consequences of his friendship. One only has to look around to notice that Devil devotees may be found in all walks of life, from the mightiest king to the craftiest peasant. It would appear that the Dark One is still having his day by the preponderance of satanists, sorcerers, diviners, and magicians (let alone your run-of-the-mill sinners) that populate this world. To those who believe strict Christian doctrine, anyone who does not believe that Christ died to redeem our souls is under the Devil's spell, regardless of his or her virtue. In fact it is a common trait in religions to diabolize anyone who does not espouse precisely the same faith, and Christianity is only

Last Judgement
(detail), by Giotto di
Bondone, 1305–1310

145

one example. For a long time, people thought that remarkable talent or a positive reversal in fortune in a neighbor was a sign the Devil was afoot. Insanity, deformity, red hair, left-handedness, refusals to attend church, stammering during prayer, even an ability to tame animals fell under suspicious eyes ever alert for demonic activity. Whatever the case, one thing seems true: His Satanic Majesty does tend to lurk about, patiently waiting for one little human slip. He will often go to great lengths to secure a person's loyalty—signing blood contracts, granting impossible wishes, endowing fabulous gifts—in an effort to cheat God out of yet another soul. Satan can offer tremendous power, wealth, and pleasure for those who consort with him in life, but the price is most certainly dear.

Satanists:

The most familiar form of devil worship, and the one most ballyhooed in the media, are the cults of faithful who adore the Christian Devil *because* he is evil and represents an alternative, powerful—albeit negative—force. These particular fans of the Prince can be as dedicated as believers in other forms of religion, congregating regularly, participating in their own customized Black Mass, and writing their own liturgy. It is commonly believed that some gruesome activity is involved in these rituals. Some reportedly drink real blood; others steal consecrated hosts from churches and blaspheme them. Some sects profane the Passion of Christ by worshipping an upside down crucifix or trampling the cross. One common theme is the live

A ritual sacrifice performed by witches

sacrifice of some small animal. In certain satanic sects, priests allegedly copulate with acolytes on a dedicated altar. Satanists, in opposi-
tion to the emphasis church fathers put on mind and spirit, are said
to believe and encourage free love and body worship. The five-sided
star, or pentangle, is a popular symbol of occult religion and has long
been used as a type of graffiti by Satanists. The organization of Free-

*Lucifer before
the Fall*

masons was accused of Satanism by the Roman Catholic church for years, a charge they vehemently denied.

There are other signifigant groups of believers who are proud to be called devil worshippers because their deity *is* Lucifer. Some creeds believe he was unjustly punished; others think he was tricked by the archangel Michael out of spite and jealousy. They see Lucifer as an embodiment of *good* banished for no reason, and they have their own creation stories to prove it. Devil worship of this nature stems from early dualistic religions, such as the Persian belief in Ahriman, the embodiment of chaos, and Orzud, the embodiment of creation. Many gnostic sects continued this idea of opposing forces during the early years of Christianity until their leaders were persecuted as heretics. Although this dualism does not seem to challenge the Christian idea of God and the Devil, two supernatural powers battling for humanity, traditional Christians believe it is blasphemy to compare any entity's might with God's because God is all powerful and any calamity the Devil besets on the world occurs only because God, who sees the big picture, allows it to be so.

The horned god of witches

Sorcerers and Magicians:
If the witch is the Devil's harem girl, then the sorcerer is his friend and playmate. While witches must do what they are told to keep their powers, sorcerers, who are predominantly male, sell their souls to the Devil in exchange for learning his art. According to the *grimoires* that exist today, most sorcerers hoped to use their knowledge to harness the nature of evil and force the

The Devil and

Saint Patrick

Prince of Darkness to do *their* bidding. And what did these jackanapes want? Great opulence, power, and wisdom, of course, to cheat the Devil out of their souls—an astonishingly easy thing to do (see Pacts with the Devil, page 152). With a little help from the Devil, sorcerers learn the black magic embedded in colors, crystals, precious gems, and powders. They consort with demons to excite tempests, arouse virgins, fly through the air, open every door without a key, demolish buildings, ruin fortunes, and cause hatred and strife between men. To render themselves invisible, sorcerers use an ointment made from the incinerated flesh of newborn infants mixed with the blood of nightbirds. Dr. Faustus was a sorcerer, as was Merlin.

Magicians are a breed apart from sorcerers because they reject any dealings with the Devil (except, of course, for black magicians) and prefer to use physical phenomena and science to achieve their goals. Magicians, who are closer to mystics than Satanists, were not persecuted in the same way witches and sorcerers were (although they were imprisoned). In fact, many significant sages of old professed to dabble in magic, believing it to be a kind of religion in its own right. Cornelius Agrippa and Paracelsus were two renowned medieval magicians. Nevertheless, magicians were not entirely benevolent. It was said that if a black magician knew your name you would be at his mercy. If he procured a piece of your clothing or hair, he could inflict pain or disease, even kill you. Both sorcerers and magicians are indebted to the Cabala, an ancient Jewish book of mysticism, science, and magical arts whispered by God into Adam's ear. It has been passed down from the dawn of time by oral tradition. From it, sorcerers, magicians, and witches learn their magic spells, chants, and incantations.

The god of alchemy raising the philosopher's fire to the temperature of fusion

Alchemists and Diviners: Alchemy is the science by

which practitioners attempt to transmute base metals into gold. The equivalent of early chemists or apothecaries, alchemists believed gold to be the purest medicine, the most evolved substance, and a metal that could prolong life and aid the spirit toward a higher accord with supernatural spheres. Interested in healing, life extension, and enlightenment, alchemists have a faith centered around an ornate, detailed

cosmology. Alchemists were demonized for their alternative beliefs and their ability to transform matter—a job only God or demons could do. The alchemist proved his diabolical intentions by creating an artificial life form: the homunculus. This creature was conceived in a stoppered test tube and left to mature in a ripe horse-dung heap for forty weeks. An ethereal, transparent entity at birth, the homunculus, if fed by the alchemists with human blood, would emerge from the manure hill the size of a small child. He could then be raised in human fashion.

Diviners were a branch of sorcerers who could tell the future and interpret the past. They were often consulted to aid in finding hidden treasure or to prophesy. They could tell the future from almost any substance. Aside from the more common oracles of dreams, clouds, and handwriting, diviners prophesied with arithromancy, which was used to tell people's fortunes through numbers, and aeromancy, which called forth spirits of the air. Diviners used captomancy to read signs from smoke and carromancy to interpret the patterns of melting wax. Two ghastly techniques were necromancy, or divination from freshly unearthed corpses, and antinopomancy or prophesy using the entrails of women and children. Gourmet diviners could tell the future from ripening cheese, figs, and the sounds of the stomach and bowels. It was assumed that diviners learned the future by consulting with demons. They were frowned upon for trying to emulate God by predicting, and thus influencing, events—a presumptuous and wicked craft.

The Devil dances in an empty pocket

The devil totes souls to Hell in his sack

Pacts with the Devil: Anyone, if they have the nerve, can make a deal with the Devil. In exchange for one's immortal soul, the Baker will grant any wish. The best time to find the Devil is at midnight at a crossroad. If that fails, try looking in a mirror and calling him. Asking the Devil to appear is not to be taken lightly, however. Selling one's soul is obviously the quickest way to get to Hell; but if you believe what you read, humans have been doing it for as long as the Devil has been there to talk to. Writings of people who exchanged their soul for earthly success and pleasure predate the fourth century. Among the most famous tales, of course, are those about Dr. Faustus (see page 158) and Daniel Webster.

In a less dangerous tradition, people still bribe the spirits in the hope of a favor. In Nordic traditions, it is common for farmers to leave sweets or other treats to tempt the sprites into doing a little field work for them. In much the same way, we leave cookies for Santa Claus in hopes that he will leave us more presents. However, dealing with the Devil is a much more serious affair. Pacts are signed in blood, the symbol of life; and that is exactly what is at stake, at least *eternal* life. In most devilish deeds, a human sells his soul (given to him by God to do what with it he will) in exchange for the realization of his wildest desires. Money, love, power, leisure: all are his for a set period of time, usually twenty-four years. At the end of this time the Devil will come a-calling, and you had better be home.

The Devil makes false promises to his devotees

The end is nearly always painful and gruesome. As the clock strikes midnight on the appointed day, the Devil appears for his pound of flesh—which is exactly what he gets. Demons rip into skin with their talons, grab the screaming soul (often represented as a shadow), and stuff it in a bag, cackling their way back to Hell. The soul is forever-more bound in servitude to the Devil. One ultimately fiendish wrinkle: a person can sell the soul of someone else for the same riches. Parents often did this with their children, or husbands with wives.

It was quite common, however, to cheat the Devil out of his end of the deal. Once the person's time is up, he falls to his knees in prayer asking God and the saints to preserve him. Theosophilus, one of the first mortals to strike a deal with the forces of evil, repented at the last minute and prayed vehemently to the Virgin Mary for his salva-tion. With the demons scratching at his door, Mary came to him in a vision and forgave him. Theosophilus was saved and went on to live a fine upstanding life. The Devil may only take a soul who has renounced God. For being the Master of Lies, the Devil is scrupulously honest in holding up his side of the deal. He never hesitates in granting a human's wishes and patiently waits until his time arrives. Humans, however, always seem to get out of the deal, either with prayer or by hedging the terms of the pact.

Possession and Exorcism

Once in a while, people may find themselves at the mercy of the Devil without having asked for it. Sensing a weak or injured soul, a demon will grab the opportunity to jump inside the human's shell and take over. Possession is different than being harassed by demons, as the evil spirit actually inhabits its victim's body until it is exorcised. If a victim is left unexorcised, the exhausting battle between the demon and the victim's soul will eventually lead to death.

Methods of Possession: Demons (acting for the Devil)

enter the body through any orifice that is not protected. They will leap onto food about to be eaten or besiege the sleep of those who forget to cross themselves before climbing into bed. Occasionally, demons are given permission by God to enter an unsuspecting body on their own volition. More often, a witch induces an unclean spirit to take possession of a person through an incantation. Attacks are strongest when the victim is depressed, alone, afraid, or poor. When a body is possessed, it no longer owns its faculties and cannot fight the demon raging inside; the physical shell is at the utter mercy of the Devil and is not responsible for its actions.

Demons sensing a weak or injured soul will take the opportunity to possess it

Symptoms of Possession: Those possessed

desire disgusting food, but vomit it all back up upon consumption. Experiencing a heavy weight in the stomach that causes one to vomit and defecate incessantly is not uncommon. Other victims feel continous or gnawing pain in different parts of their bodies, especially the belly; the heart feels pierced by nails, the head shattered and swollen. Some spirits sap the vitality and strength from their victim, leaving the body a shadow of what it was. Others cause the possessed to display superhuman strength. Melancholy to the point of muteness and a fear of sacred objects are sure signs of demonic possession, as is a yellow, ashen color in the face and foaming at the mouth. Restless demons are not content to sit in the possessed body. Tossing about maniacally, they will throw the person across the room or make them fall if they are standing and tip over if they are seated. The victim writhes as if in agony and yells out obscenities, gibberish, or secret information in an eerily deep tone—the voice of the Devil. Possessions often occur in clusters within a community, like an epidemic, and convents and monasteries are especially prone. Animals and inanimate objects can also be possessed.

Cures: The only hope for a possessed person is a courageous priest who will perform an exorcism. If the priest is unsure of a possession, he places his hand on the person's head and lays his stole across the body. The subject, if possessed, will recoil in fear. In the prescribed rites of exorcism (which on occasion can last for days), the priest lays his hand on the body of the victim and commands the Devil to discharge his spirits. The priest then calls to the spirits and asks how many are possessing the body. If there is an answer, possession is confirmed.

Heresy is the devil's bellow.
MARTIN LUTHER

The priest asks the names of the demons and why they chose to possess this hapless soul. The priest determines the hour the demons entered the body and how long they plan to stay. At that moment, the priest calls upon the name of the Lord and demands that the demon show himself and leave the mortal alone, beginning with the phrase "God the Father commands thee. Therefore adjured in his holy name, depart from this man, whom he has created." The demons may flee at this point, but it frequently takes hours of prayer and anointment to coax the squatters out of the body of the possessed.

A priest evicts a possessing demon

Ridding a body of a demon is a complicated and dangerous business. The priest must protect himself from falling under the spell of the demon (especially perilous when exorcising a young maiden) or having his own body possessed when the demon ricochets out of the victim's flesh. Fumigation, flagellation, salt, and holy water are also used in exorcisms, since the Devil can't abide the odor or objects of sanctity. Sometimes a holy person will physically wrestle a demon from a body. Luring the demon out through the nose, ear, or mouth, the priest grabs hold of it and then manually drags it out of the body—an excruciating process for the possessed. Once free of the demon, it is not uncommon for the possessed to have no recollection of the events that transpired.

The Wolf's Gate

The cathedral at Aix-la-Chapelle in France was completed through a pact with the Devil. Emperor Charlemagne had dedicated much of his time and resources to finishing the cathedral quickly, and his last order upon leaving the city to do battle with the Saxons was that he expected the cathedral to be finished by the time he came back. The cost of that war was so immense that work on the cathedral ground to a halt. The citizens were at their wits' end, unable to complete the structure without any funds. In desperation, they swore they would get money, even if they had to borrow it from the Devil himself. The Archfiend always knows a good offer when he hears it, and almost instantly a rich stranger riding a beautiful steed arrived in town with the offer of a loan—under the simple condition that the first soul to enter the building would be forfeited to the Devil. Charlemagne was staunchly opposed to any diabolical dabblings; but, weighing his law against his wrath, the citizens decided to borrow the money. Gold and silver suddenly rained from the sky, making puddles around their feet. As the story leaked out, townspeople went into a panic wondering who would be sacrificed to give the Devil his due. After agonizing, someone came up with a brilliant plan to snare a wolf and lead it through the gate first. This they did, and the Devil took the bait and leaped on the wolf, tearing out its soul. The moment he realized he'd been the victim of a hoax, the Devil was humiliated. In his embarassment, he rushed out of the cathedral in such a huff that he slammed the door on his thumb. A bronze statue was erected by the door, known to this day as "The Wolf's Gate."

A nobleman bargains with the Devil

Dr. Faust

The most famous pact made with the Devil is that by Dr. Faust (or in some versions, Dr. Faustus). The theme of the Faust legend has been written and rewritten by many authors in several cultures and mythologized as a result of Goethe's popular rendition, entitled *Faust.* There is little doubt that Dr. Faust was a real person who lived in the early sixteenth century in eastern Europe. He was a man of strange habits, a self-professed occultist who always traveled in the company of a younger man named Wagner and a small black dog he had taught to fetch food. When his body was found one morning, ripped apart and tossed on a manure hill outside the town of Wittenburg, neighbors speculated that Faust had met his grisly end when the Devil came to collect on a bargain. The local doctor declared, officially, that the Devil had wrung Dr. Faust's neck. In the many stories and dramas that were inspired by these

Dr. Faust applies his diabolical powers

events, Faust is often portrayed as a man hungry for knowledge, understanding, and power who sells his soul to Mephistopheles for twenty-four years. In Goethe's version, Faust is saved by a woman named Gretchen and taken away by angels only moments before he is to be packed off to Hell.

Protection

With the air thick with demons, the Devil stalking your every move, a witch living next door, and the gates of Hell yawning ever wider with each minor trespass, how can mere mortals arm themselves against the constant onslaught of evil? Luckily the Devil and his legions are not invincible. A person is most at risk during birth, when traveling alone at night, while sleeping, and during death. Evil spirits love to traumatize new-born infants and corpses, and relatives of both should take extra steps to ensure their safety. It is always a good idea to know your enemy and then take the necessary precautions. A few home remedies, common sense, and a lucky charm will offer enough of a deterrent to send the bogeymen on their way. As long as people have believed in the Devil and the forces of evil, they have created charms, amulets, and talismans to fend him off. Charms are chants recited by priests and believers to ward off the Devil and bring good luck. A charm can also be an activity that, once done, will keep away bad spirits. An amulet is a natural object worn or held by a person to ward off evil and bad luck. It can also be nailed to a door or piece of furniture. Talismans are amulets that require you to do something such as wave it, kiss it, or rub it to repel wicked spirits. The best defense, of course, is a pure heart and a clean spirit, but if you can't claim ownership of these two weapons at all times you might want to try a few of the following.

To eat an apple without rubbing it first is to challenge the Devil.

Charms: The following activities are age-old precautions against evil and can be modified depending on the power of the offending spirit. The easiest charm of all is to recite the Lord's Prayer (or any prayer). Chanting a saint's hymn or multiplying the gospels will also work. The word *abracadabra,* an ancient and magical incantation to fortify oneself against evil, is actually the name of a spirit. When you recite its name, it will come protect you. Calling aloud to a saint when set upon by demons will put them at bay. It is best if you know who your patron saint is or what saints' day it is. The more specific you are, the better. The odor of sanctity—unwashed, unshaven monks, for example—scares the Devil, as does the smell of incense. The infamous Brother Juniper, who took the vows of Saint Francis to their fullest degree, had such rank body odor that even the mention of his name was enough to make any demon blanch and run away. Thus, his name is a guaranteed protection.

A saint grabs a thieving devil by the nose

The sound of ringing bells is cacophony to demons. They hate it. The reason one rings bells before church is to dispel all the evil spirits from the vicinity. Bells were placed around the necks of livestock to ward off evil spirits. The death of a Christian is accompanied by ringing bells to ensure a safe passage into the afterlife. Weddings and baptisms are also heralded by bells because demons love to ruin happy occasions. Making the sign of the cross (which is easily done by crossing two fingers) and reciting the holy name of the Lord will expel the Devil. Sprinkling holy water or salt does the trick as well. Salt is a preservative, an extender of life, and the Devil is afraid of it. Lighting candles or tapers is also good protection. Since demons love to nest in dark places, a lighted candle dispels them. Burning incense or sage, or fumigating the house with sulfur, offends their nostrils. An ointment derived from the gallbladder of a black dog will protect a house if it is smeared on the thresholds and walls.

Drawing a protective circle and standing in its center will provide a shield through which demons cannot cross. If that is impossible, spinning around in a clockwise circle three times will force the ghouls to leave. Circles are considered sacred because they represent the eternal cycle of life and the power of the sun. If a witch has a circle drawn around her, don't enter it or you will be her captive. The same is true for fairy rings. Unless you get permission, entering a fairy ring can lead to death. Wearing the color blue is a good precaution—diabolical spirits don't like blue because it is the color of Heaven.

Devils expelled from Arezzo

Martin Luther recommended dealing with evil spirits directly. Farting in the Devil's face may seem rude, but it will make him leave. Kicking, punching, and dragging demons around is also effective. An ink blot still visible on the wall of Martin Luther's house in Wittenberg comes from the time he threw his ink bottle at a demon who was hounding him.

He who sups with the Devil should have a long spoon.

Amulets:
Amulets can be carried or worn as armor against marauding spirits. (Children and animals also benefit from amulets, which protect them from the Evil Eye.) Placing an amulet at a threshold will stop the Devil at the door. Red peppers are used in Italy to dispel unclean spirits. A red thread tied around a finger will also work. Saints' relics offer particularly good protection if you can manage to carry a piece of one. Coral is good at repelling demons and the vagaries of the Evil Eye. It will also guard against nightmares. The four-leaf clover is a very lucky amulet. It is thought to be one of the few plants Adam and Eve took from the Garden of Eden. Horseshoes are powerful against evil; their crescent shape and seven nail holes are good weapons. If you hang a horseshoe prongs up, the Devil will get sucked into it as he approaches your house. Prongs down and the power of the horseshoe pours out into a force field protecting the house. Horses are protected just by wearing their shoes. Knots catch evil spirits at the spot where the knot is tied. Priests wear a clerical collar due to the fear that demons would get tangled in a tie and disrupt religious services. The Star of

Saint Dunstan and the Devil

David, or Solomon's Seal, is extremely forceful against evil. If you are being chased by demons, draw one and hold it against your chest.

Plants and herbs such as betony, pimpernel, vervain, henbane, rosemary, sage, St. John's Wort, and leaves from bay and oak trees have special powers against evil. If you sense any untoward goings-on in your vicinity, wear a sprig of one of these plants in your lapel.

Talismans: Rubbing a rabbit's foot or wishing on an eyelash are both popular uses for good-luck talismans. Any object that you touch or activate in any way is considered a talisman. Because doors are an open invitation to the Devil, door knockers often have images of lions, gargoyles, or angels on them that ensure a demon will not enter when your guest does. Knocking on wood keeps evil away. Saints' medallions and crucifixes are both extremely effective when rubbed or kissed. Making a daisy chain and wearing it will catch demons in its links. Gems that ward off evil when rubbed are sapphires, topaz, pearls, and opals.

St. John's Wort has special powers against evil

Popular Superstitions:

Certain people with special powers can tell whether someone is lying by the demons cavorting on the person's tongue.

Farmers in Scotland always left a portion of their field fallow and dedicated it to the Devil, believing the rest of their farm would be more productive.

Sudden hot or cold drafts are a sign the Devil is around. A hot draft on a summer day is air from Hell escaping into the earth.

The north door in some churches in England is called the Devil's door. It is left open during baptisms so the Devil can flee.

In Ireland, people surround a dead body with twelve burning candles to keep it safe from marauding demons.

In the sixteenth century, it was widely believed that people who had eyebrows that grew together were evil.

Parsley is so hard to grow it is commonly said that it goes to Hell and back before germinating. For this reason, anyone who has a patch of healthy parsley growing in their yard might be in league with the Devil.

*The Devil and Saint
Cuthbert*

According to Pliny, nails extracted from a tomb and driven into a threshold will guard against nightmares.

Friday is the day of the week when demons run rampant. One should never begin a voyage or new enterprise on Friday, especially a marriage. If you have been ill, don't get up for the first time on Friday.

If you throw salt over your left shoulder, you will sting the Devil's eyes. Spitting over your left shoulder will stop a pursuing demon in his tracks. Wearing your clothes inside out will confuse him.

Always get out of bed on the right side, as it is common knowledge that evil spirits prefer the left side. They will lurk by the bed waiting to hang on to you if you exit from their side. It is also a good idea to cross yourself before bed, especially if you happen to be a virgin.

Cutting your nails or hair on Sunday means the Devil will visit you all week.

The Devil will enter your mouth when you yawn, so it is wise to cross your fingers when you cover your mouth.

In the morning, wash your face and hands with fresh cold water. Then throw the wash water as far as you can out the window or door. Apparently, evil spirits must stop where the water lands.

Never enter a friend's home with your left foot first unless you want to bring the Devil in with you.

> *Let love be genuine; hate what is evil, hold fast to what is good.*
> ROMANS 12:9

BIBLIOGRAPHY

Carus, Paul. *The History of the Devil.* Chicago: The Open Court Publishing Company, 1900.

Davidson, Gustav. *A Dictionary of Angels.* New York: The Free Press, 1967.

Gardiner, Eileen, ed. *Visions of Heaven & Hell before Dante.* New York: Italica Press, 1989.

Godwin, Malcolm. *Angels.* New York: Simon & Schuster, 1990.

Hackins, J. *Asiatic Mythology.* New York: Thomas Y. Crowell Co., 1974.

Maple, Eric. *The Domain of Devils.* London: Robert Hale, 1966.

Masello, Robert. *Fallen Angels.* New York: Perigee Books, 1994.

Melton, J. Gordon. *An Encyclopedic Handbook of Cults in America.* New York & London: Garland Publishing, Inc., 1992.

Milton, John. *The Complete Prose and Poetry of John Milton.* New York: Random House, 1942.

Opie, Iona and Moira Tatem, eds. *A Dictionary of Superstitions.* Oxford: Oxford University Press, 1989.

Pinsky, Robert. *The Inferno of Dante.* New York: Farrar, Straus and Giroux, 1994.

Potter, Carole. *Knock on Wood & Other Superstitions: An Encyclopedia of Talismans, Charms, Superstitions & Symbols.* New York: Bonanza Books, 1983.

Robbins, Russell Hope. *The Encyclopedia of Witchcraft and Demonology.* New York: Crown Publishers, 1959.

Rony, Jérôme-Antoine. *A History of Magic.* New York: Walker and Company, 1950.

Rudwin, Maximilian. *The Devil in Legend and Literature.* Chicago: The Open Court Publishing Company, 1959.

Russell, Jeffrey Burton. *Lucifer: The Devil in the Middle Ages.* Ithaca: Cornell University Press, 1984.

———. *The Prince of Darkness: Radical Evil and the Power of Good in History.* Ithaca: Cornell University Press, 1988.

Spence, Lewis, ed. *An Encyclopedia of Occultism.* New York: Carol Publishing Group, 1990.

The Holy Bible, Revised Standard Version. King James Translation.

Wall, J. Charles. *Devils.* London: Methuen & Co., 1904.

ART SOURCES

Cover: *Last Judgement* (right panel) by Hans Memling, Narodowe Museum, Gdansk, Poland, Erich Lessing/Art Resource, New York.

Page 6: *Saint Francis of Borgia Exorcising a Demonized Dying Man*, Francisco de Goya y Lucientes, 1788, Cathedral, Valencia, Spain, Giraudon/Art Resource, New York.

Page 9: *Devil Dog* © William Wegman, 1990, Courtesy PaceWildensteinMacGill Gallery, New York, NY.

Page 35: *Last Judgement* by Fra Angelico, Museum of San Marco, Florence, Italy, Scala/Art Resource, New York.

Page 40: *Lucifer* by Tintoretto (detail from *The Temptation of Christ*) Scuola di Rocco, Venice, Scala/Art Resource, New York.

Page 67: *The Inferno* by Jean Columbe (from *Très Riches Heures du duc de Berry*), Musée Condé, Chantilly, France, Giraudon/Art Resource, New York.

Page 72: *The Damned in Hell* (detail) by Luca Signorelli, Duomo, Orvieto, Scala/Art Resource, New York.

Page 80: Diagram of Dante's *Inferno*, Illustration by Brenda Rae Eno.

Page 107: *Fragment of the Last Judgement* by Hieronymus Bosch, uncertain dating, (60 x 114), Alte Pinakothek, Munich, Germany, Giraudon/Art Resource, New York.

Page 104: *Last Judgement* (detail) by Giotto di Bondone, Scrovegni Chapel, Padua, Scala/Art Resource, New York.

Page 110: *The Temptation of St. Anthony* by Grünewald (from the *Isenheim Altarpiece*), Unterlinden Museum, Colmar, Giraudon/Art Resource, New York.

Page 130: *Witches' Sabbath* by Francisco Goya, 16 1/2" x 11 3/4", Museo Lazaro Galdiano, Madrid, Spain, Giraudon/Art Resource, New York.

Mara, enemy of Buddha

The Devil is never far off.

Following page:
Satan in paradise, by
Gustave Doré, 19th
century engraving